THE PUFFIN BOOK C

Also in this series

THE PUFFIN BOOK OF HORSE AND PONY STORIES
THE PUFFIN BOOK OF SCHOOL STORIES
THE PUFFIN BOOK OF FUNNY STORIES
THE PUFFIN BOOK OF GHOSTS AND GHOULS
THE PUFFIN BOOK OF SCIENCE FICTION

The Puffin Book of
Song and Dance

STORIES CHOSEN BY
JAN MARK

PUFFIN BOOKS

PUFFIN BOOKS

Published by the Penguin Group
Penguin Books Ltd, 27 Wrights Lane, London W8 5TZ, England
Penguin Books USA Inc., 375 Hudson Street, New York, New York 10014, USA
Penguin Books Australia Ltd, Ringwood, Victoria, Australia
Penguin Books Canada Ltd, 10 Alcorn Avenue, Toronto, Ontario, Canada M4V 3B2
Penguin Books (NZ) Ltd, 182–190 Wairau Road, Auckland 10, New Zealand

Penguin Books Ltd, Registered Offices: Harmondsworth, Middlesex, England

First published by Viking 1992
Published in Puffin Books 1994
1 3 5 7 9 10 8 6 4 2

This collection copyright © Jan Mark, 1992
All rights reserved

The acknowledgements on pages 169 and 170 constitute an extension of this copyright page

Printed in England by Clays Ltd, St Ives plc
Filmset in Bembo

Except in the United States of America, this book is sold subject
to the condition that it shall not, by way of trade or otherwise, be lent,
re-sold, hired out, or otherwise circulated without the publisher's
prior consent in any form of binding or cover other than that in
which it is published and without a similar condition including this
condition being imposed on the subsequent purchaser

Contents

Introduction

If you write books or paint pictures or carve statues it can be weeks, months or even years before anyone sees what you have created, by which time you will be somewhere else, creating something else. With the performing arts, such as music, dancing and drama, you are watched. Whatever it is that you do, you need an audience. (No one ever paid good money to watch an author writing a book.)

Melanie, in 'The Poppycrunch Kid' by Adèle Geras, has an audience: the millions of people who see the commercial that she appears in, and one other – the camera. The children from *The Enchanted Castle* by E. Nesbit are so desperate for an audience to watch their play that they *make* one, while in Richmal Crompton's 'William Holds the Stage' William himself ignores the entire audience and the rest of the cast, to act only for the girl of his dreams, in the second row.

Although William is only appearing in a school

play, he does at least have a stage to hold. The very earliest miracle plays were performed on a cart, like the one in *A Little Lower than the Angels*. This extract is taken from a book by Geraldine McCaughrean, about a stonemason's apprentice who joins a company of travelling players.

Another strange setting for a performance is the haunted hillock overlooking a river in 'Hear My Voice' by Dennis Hamley, while Adrian Alington's 'The Man who Understood Cats' takes place in an ordinary theatre, being the story of a man who spent his life playing Dick Whittington's cat in panto-mimes.

People who become professional performers spend their lives in training, long past the point where they seem to us to have achieved perfection. The story about the practice session of a string quartet comes from *The Facts and Fictions of Minna Pratt* by Patricia MacLachlan, a novel about an American girl who is studying to become a cellist. Minna has every encouragement, but Karen Forrest, who has a disastrous first public performance, is a talented pianist who comes from a totally unmusical family. Her very real struggle to become a professional concert pianist is told in the novel *She Shall Have Music* by Kitty Barne. The lads in Michelle Magorian's 'The Greatest' have a hard road ahead of them before they realize their ambition to be dancers, and the extract from *A Swarm in May*, one of four books by William Mayne about a choir school, gives some idea of the work put in by the boys who sing the services in a cathedral.

And there is someone who does not act or dance or sing. Anna comes from a family of American gospel singers, but she is the one without a voice who has to stand at the back and sell records and tapes to the audience after a show. Her story is told in *The Glory Girl* by Betsy Byars.

Jan Mark

The Poppycrunch Kid

ADÈLE GERAS

'OK, my darling, let me just explain what I want
you to do and then we'll rehearse it a couple of
times before we try it on camera. Right?'

Melanie nodded. Bill, the producer, was being nice
to her. Much nicer than he was to everyone else in the
studio. He shouted at them sometimes, swore even.
But he never shouted or swore at her, because she was
the Poppycrunch Kid and Very Important.

Melanie pulled her skirt down and fluffed out her
bunches. Were her ribbons still all right? Mum said
she was a Star. It was hard to believe. Two weeks
ago, she'd lined up with a whole lot of other little
girls and they'd chosen her out of all of them to be
the Poppycrunch Kid. Some of the girls had been
much prettier, too.

'But your little girl, Mrs White,' Bill had said to
her mother and right in front of her, too, 'has such
zest, such life, such – how shall I put it? – spice, that's

the word, the right word – the others were all – d'you know what I mean? – flavourless. And, you see, what the makers do want to promote more than anything is an image of Brightness, Vigour and Intelligence ... the concept is one of Life, you see, rather than an unreal kind of prettiness. I'm sure Melanie will be Perfection Itself.'

Melanie didn't understand why the sight of her trampolining, skipping, sliding down a helter-skelter, leaping out of bed or doing a tap-dance, dressed always in a red T-shirt and a short white skirt, should make everyone stop buying their favourite cereal and turn to Poppycrunch instead. *She* wasn't going to eat it.

'But you must,' said Mrs White in desperation.

'Why?'

'It's called Brand Loyalty. They're paying you enough money. You might at least do them the favour of eating their cereal. I think it's lovely.'

'It's horrible. All hard. I could think up a few truthful slogans, like "Tear your gums on a Poppy-crunch", or something.'

'But you're going to be famous, Melanie. Don't you want to be famous? Isn't that what you've always wanted? You've said so over and over again. "I want to be a star", you said.'

'It's not being a star – not advertising cereal. I want to be in a proper show, like *Annie*. I wish I'd got into *Annie*.'

'You were too tall. I keep telling you. And besides,

millions more people see advertisements than ever walk into a theatre. Maybe someone'll spot you. You never know. Anyway, it's good exposure, you've got to say that for it.'

That was the only reason Melanie could think of for doing it. Someone, someone from Hollywood even, would see her trampolining or skipping or whatever, and decide, right there on the spot, that she was exactly what he needed for his very next film and whisk her far away in a jet to be a real actress, a child star.

'Are you ready, Melanie?' Bill cooed.

'Yes.'

'Right. Let's start then.'

Melanie skipped towards the trampoline (red, with 'Poppycrunch' written on it in white letters), leaped on to it and began to bounce, singing at the same time the silly little tune they'd given her to learn, and smiling widely enough to crack her face open:

> Full of goodness
> Full of fun
> Poppycrunch
> The chewy one!

Three things at once – it was harder to do than it looked, like patting your head with one hand while rubbing the other hand over your stomach in circles. Melanie had to do it four times before she'd got it just right. At last, Bill was satisfied.

'Great, my love,' he said. 'Absolutely scrumptious.

Now, as soon as you've got your breath back, we'll film it. OK?'

'Yes,' said Melanie. The thought of doing it all over again on film made the butterflies start up in her stomach, just as though she were about to act in front of a real, live audience. It was silly. There was only Bill and Christine, his assistant, and some lighting men and sound men and her mother in the corner of the studio and, of course, the cameras. Melanie had never thought about the cameras before. They were like robots: huge square tall things on long metal legs that slid across the floor trailing thick black cables like snakes. You had to look at them quite hard to spot the men who were working them. The cameras had lenses for eyes sticking out towards you. Never, never looking at anything else except you. Melanie shivered.

'Now, Melanie, I don't want you to think about the cameras at all. Just forget about them. They're not there, all right? I want you to be quite, quite natural, my love, and Reg and Ben here will do all the work – focus on you like mad, all the time. Give Melanie a little wave, lads, just to show her you're there.'

Arms came out of the sides of the cameras and waved. It was as if the cameras themselves were waving at her.

'Righto, my dears,' said Bill. 'If you're all ready I'm going to do my Cecil B. de Mille routine . . . Roll 'em!'

Melanie sang and smiled and trampolined. She sang and smiled and trampolined seven times. They had to do seven 'takes' before everything came out exactly as Bill wanted it.

'That's fantastic, Melanie. Really fantastic. It's not unknown for me to do a dozen takes. Great. It's going to look great. Come and see.'

Melanie went. It seemed like a lot of other advertisements to her. She was quite pleased with how high she'd managed to jump on the trampoline, but it was all over so quickly – a few seconds, that was all. Tomorrow they would do leaping out of bed. That shouldn't be so tiring. Suddenly Melanie felt exhausted, unable to think straight. The silly words and silly tune of the Poppycrunch jingle had got stuck in her head and wound round her other thoughts like thin strings of chewing-gum that wouldn't come off.

> Full of goodness
> Full of fun
> Poppycrunch
> The chewy one.

Round and round in her head.

That night, Melanie dreamed that Camera One was in her bedroom. Standing in the doorway and looking at her room. And there was a wind. It blew all round the room and sucked the furniture and the toys and all her dolls and clothes and the pictures from the walls till everything was whirling round and round in a spiral that started out huge and got smaller and smaller until at last it vanished right into the lens of the camera and then the walls weren't there any longer either, just a bed with her in it, and Camera One floating about in a bright, colourless space that went on and on for ever and never stopped.

'Christine,' said Melanie, 'do you think you could ask Bill something for me?'

'Of course, poppet. Anything you like. What is it?'

'Well, it's a bit embarrassing . . .'

'Go on, you can tell me. Can't you? You know I'll help.'

'Yes, I know, but it's so stupid.'

'Never mind, it's obviously worrying you, so go ahead and tell me. You'll feel better, honestly.'

'It's Camera One. I'm scared of it.'

'Scared of a camera?' Christine smiled. 'But why, love? What do you think it can do to you?'

'I don't know. I dreamed about it, that's all.'

'You're overwrought, my love. Don't worry. You're frightened because it's new to you. It's . . . well . . . it's a bit like stage fright, only different. Come and have a look. I'll get Reg to let you touch it and get to know it so you'll never be frightened of it again.'

Reg was understanding.

'It's only a kind of mechanical eye, love. That's all. Metal and glass and stuff that can see. It is a bit like magic, I grant you, because it's a clever old thing. Does a lot that your eyes and mine can't do – it can give back the pictures that it sees and show them all over again but it's not magic, see. It's called Technology. Nothing to be scared of, honestly.'

'No, I suppose not,' said Melanie. 'I'm being stupid.'

'No, no, love,' said Reg. 'It's not stupid. I'll tell you something. There are primitive tribes in the world, New Guinea and places like that, who don't even like snapshots being taken of them. They reckon every time a photo gets taken, it steals away a bit of their soul. That's their superstition, see? Bet you've had a million snapshots taken of you since you were born, and you're none the worse for it, are you? Neither is anyone else. So don't worry, OK?'

'OK,' said Melanie and went over to the beautiful bed that had been set out on the studio floor. I wish Reg hadn't told me that, she thought. About those people in New Guinea. I know it's only a superstition, but I wish he hadn't told me, all the same.

'Action!' Bill shouted and Melanie bounded out of bed, grinning and singing:

> Ready for work
> Ready for play
> Start every day
> The Poppycrunch way!

She did it ten times. It wasn't her fault. They had to find some way of getting the pillow into the picture with her. The famous Poppycrunch symbol was printed on the pillowslip and, of course, it had to be seen, or what was the point?

There were three more films to make. The helter-skelter was fun. A very short tune and not a lot of words:

> Bite it
> Munch it
> Poppycrunch it!

Also, Melanie didn't care how many times she had to come sliding down till the timing was just perfect. She was getting used to filming, beginning to enjoy it, just as Bill and Christine and Reg had said she would. She sang the songs at home, all the time. At school, she showed her friends exactly what she had to do. She found it very hard to concentrate on her work, because her head was full of bouncy music and bright slogan words and they seemed to be pushing whatever it was she was supposed to be thinking about into some corner of her mind where she could never quite reach it.

Miss Hathersage, her teacher, asked her one day, 'Melanie, dear, what are seven nines?'

Melanie's mind raced. Seven nines? What were nines? Full of goodness . . . Nine whats? Sevens . . . Full of fun . . .

'I don't know, Miss.'

'Of course you know, dear. You did the nine times table last year. Now come on, dear, think.'

Melanie thought . . . the chewy one. She closed her eyes . . . white skirt flying . . . jump as high as you can . . . Poppycrunch . . . ready for work . . . ready for play . . .

'I can't think, Miss, I'm sorry.' Melanie hung her head.

'Very well, then. Some people have let being on television go to their heads, I can see. Sarah, what are seven nines?'

'Sixty-three, Miss Hathersage.'

'Quite right. Sixty-three. Do you remember now, Melanie?'

'Yes, Miss.' But I don't remember, Melanie thought. I don't and I must. Seven nines are sixty-three, sixty-three. Even as she thought it, she felt the numbers slipping away, losing their meaning, losing themselves over the precipices that seemed to lie at the very edges of her mind.

That night, Melanie dreamed that she was reading. Camera One was looking at her as she turned the pages of her book. She watched as the words flew off the page and drifted on to the floor, millions of tiny black letters, all over the rug. She tried to pick them up and put them back into the book in the right order, but they fell out of her hands, and crumbled like ash when she touched them.

'What's the matter, love?' said Christine. 'You're looking a bit pale today. Are you tired? I bet you are, you know. You've had to do all these films one on top of the other and never a rest in between. Bill,' she raised her voice, 'I'm going to take Melanie back to Make-Up. I think she needs a spot more rouge, don't you?'

Bill came and stood in front of Melanie, frowning.

'Yes, darling. Oh, and ask them at the same time to see if they can get rid of those shadows under her eyes. You've not been looking after yourself, love, now have you? You must, you know. That's what we're paying you for – to look healthy, full of life. Run along with Christine now and see what Make-Up can do for you.'

Melanie lay in the make-up chair listening to Christine's voice which seemed to come from very far away.

'I don't think you're getting enough sleep, love. Honestly. Are you?'

'I start every day the Poppycrunch way . . .' Melanie whispered.

'Are you sleeping properly, Melanie?'

'I dream a lot,' Melanie said.

'Bad dreams?' Christine sounded concerned.

'No. Poppycrunch dreams. Just me and Camera One.'

'You dream about Camera One? I thought you'd got over all that. You don't seem nervous in front of the cameras at all. What do you dream?'

'I dream I'm singing and I don't know what comes next and then Camera One looks at me and I know . . . I know what to do if it looks at me. It tells me what to say.'

'What does it tell you to say?'

'Words. Tunes.

> Poppycrunch for you
> Poppycrunch for me
> Poppycrunch for breakfast
> Poppycrunch for tea.'

'Those are today's words,' Christine sounded worried. 'I'll have a word with your mum and Bill after the filming today. I reckon you need a damned good rest. You're just exhausted. Tell me,' she added as though something had just occurred to her, 'what do you do at home? For relaxation? Do you read any books?'

'No. I stopped. I used to like it, but then I stopped.'

'Why did you stop?'

Melanie looked up. 'Because I can't remember what the story's about any more. I can't hold the story in my head. It's as though,' Melanie hesitated, 'as though my head's full of deep, black water and everything that goes in it just sinks under the water and won't come up to the surface again.'

'Right,' said Christine. 'See if you can get through this afternoon's filming and then I'll have a word with them. It won't be long now.'

'Oh,' Melanie's face lit up, 'you don't have to do that. Don't worry. I love the filming. I love Camera One. I know all the words. And all the tunes. And just what to do.' Melanie skipped all the way back to the studio, singing the Poppycrunch jingle for today. Christine followed more slowly. All hell was going to break loose when she told Bill. That was for sure.

'Christine, my beloved,' said Bill, 'you have clearly taken leave of your senses. Let me go over what you've just said. Melanie White is exhausted and overwrought and you think we should scrap the whole of the last film. Is that right?'

'Yes,' said Christine quietly. 'That's quite right.'

'Well, now, I'll answer you as calmly as I can because I don't want a row. I'll try and go over the points one by one so that you understand. First, the Poppycrunch commercials are the hottest thing I've done since the Suckamints Campaign, and you know how many prizes that won. Sales of Poppycrunch are up twenty per cent in the last two weeks. It follows, therefore, that the makers are not going to look kindly on someone jeopardizing their profits. Second, this last film is the biggest and most important of all. It's much longer. It's got fifteen other kids in it besides Melanie, doing things in the background while she dances at the front, and each one of those kids has to be cosseted and looked after, not to mention paid. It has a ten-piece band that has to be cosseted and looked after as much as the kids and paid even more. We've booked studio time. We've rehearsed, and we've even paid through our noses to be allowed to use the tune of "Sweet Georgia Brown". So I ask you, how can I cancel? Go on. Tell me. I'm anxious to know.'

Christine said nothing.

Bill went on: 'What do you think, Mrs White? Would you be in favour of cancelling? Do you think Melanie is exhausted and overwrought?'

'Well,' Mrs White considered, 'she is a bit tired, naturally. I mean, we all are, aren't we? I am myself and I just sit here and watch. But Melanie would be ever so put out if it was cancelled. I do know that. Eats, drinks and sleeps Poppycrunch, she does. Obsessed with it. Sings those tunes all day and every day. If her friends come over she teaches them all the words, tells them everything she has to do. They just play Poppycrunch games. Well, they don't come round much any more. I reckon they're fed up and I have said to her she ought to ease up a bit, but it's as if she can't. It's as if, I can't explain it really, as if there's no room left inside her for anything else.'

'Then don't you think we should stop it before it's too late?' Christine said. 'You're her mother. You can see. You've said yourself – she's obsessed.'

17

'Yes, but,' Mrs White looked down at her hands, embarrassed, 'I'm sure it'll be all right when all the filming's finished. It is only one more after all, isn't it?'

'Right,' said Bill. 'Only one more. So that's decided. I'm really glad we were able to agree, Mrs White. It's going to be a corker, this last film. Wait and see.'

That night, Melanie dreamed again. Her mother and her school friends and Bill and Christine were all standing in the television studio and one by one they went up and stood in front of Camera One. Each one of them went right up to the camera and said something and then they got smaller and smaller until they disappeared altogether. Then she went and stood right up close to Camera One and said, 'I'm the Poppy-crunch Kid,' and then she got larger and larger until she took up all the space in the studio and Camera One kept looking at her and she kept growing and growing until she was all there was left in the whole world.

Melanie knew all the words, of course, but they were written up on a big board for the benefit of the fifteen little girls who had to jiggle up and down in the background while Melanie tap-danced at the front. The only words Melanie had to sing were: 'The

Poppycrunch Kid'. She had to sing it six times and then the film ended with her singing the last three lines all on her own. This is the best of all, thought Melanie. A real band, not a tape, all those other children, and that tune, so much more zingy than the others.

'Here we go, kids,' said Bill. 'Let's try it from the top.'

The saxophone played an introduction and the children dutifully began jigging about and singing as Melanie went into the dance routine:

> Who's that kid with the bouncy step?
> *The Poppycrunch Kid!*
>   (this was Melanie's line)
> Who's the girl who's full of pep?
> *The Poppycrunch Kid!*
> Who's got the other kids all sewn up?
> *The Poppycrunch Kid!*
> *The Poppycrunch Kid!*
> You said it, you did!
>
> Who's got the shiny eyes and hair?
> *The Poppycrunch Kid!*
> When fun happens, who's right there?
> *The Poppycrunch Kid!*
> The cereal this kid eats
> Is the kind with the built-in treats . . .
> *Nuts and honey*
> *For your money*
> *Be a Poppycrunch Kid!*

It was much harder, Melanie decided, filming with all the others. So many things went wrong: someone's hair ribbon came undone, someone looked the wrong way, a wrong note came from one of the band. Any one of a thousand things could happen and did happen and they had to start again. Melanie didn't mind. She fixed her eyes on Camera One's magic eye, and felt as though just looking at it, she was falling and falling down into a place where there was nothing except light and music and tapping feet and words that circled in her brain and didn't puzzle her or worry her or make her think: words that comforted her, made her feel safe, magic words that were all she needed to say. Spells, incantations that were so powerful they could empty your head of every other thought . . .

'Twenty takes,' said Bill. 'I'm finished. Completely and utterly finished, Christine, and that's the truth.'

'You're not the only one,' said Christine. 'Did you see Melanie?'

'She's a real trouper, that kid. I mean she even looked as if she were loving every minute of it all the way through.'

'She was,' said Christine. 'It's not normal. How's she going to go back to ordinary life? I worry about it sometimes.'

'Don't be silly, love. It's not as though she's the first child ever to appear on a commercial. We've got another lot coming in tomorrow to audition for the crisps film, Lord help us.'

'No, but she was different.'

'Bloody good on camera, though,' said Bill, 'and that's what counts in the end, isn't it?'

'Oh yes,' Christine agreed dully. 'The camera just loved her. You could see that.'

On the studio floor, Camera One stood amid its cables with a plastic cover over it to protect it from the dust. Its work was finished. Until tomorrow. Until the next child was chosen.

'Hello, dear,' said the doctor. 'And how are you today?'

'Full of goodness, full of fun,' said Melanie.

'You're looking much better, I must say. Have you thought about what I asked you yesterday?'

Melanie nodded.

'Good girl. That's a good girl. Now. Tell me who you are. Tell me your name.'

'The Poppycrunch Kid.'

'No, Melanie. That's not your name, is it? Your name is Melanie White. Believe me. Say it.'

'Melanie White.'

'There, doesn't that sound better? Are you going to play today, Melanie?'

'Ready for work, ready for play, start every day the Poppycrunch way.'

'You could play outside today. It's a beautiful day.'

'I'm full of pep . . .'

'I'm glad to hear it. Your mother will be coming to see you today. That'll be nice, won't it? You love having visitors, don't you?'

'Bite it, munch it, Poppycrunch it . . .'

'I'll see you tomorrow then, Melanie.' The doctor stood up. 'I'll look in after breakfast.'

'Poppycrunch for breakfast,' said Melanie and turned over to look at the wall.

I've got shiny eyes and hair and when fun happens I'm right there, but they took Camera One away. Maybe if I'm extra good, it'll come back. I'm the kid with the bouncy step. That man. He's the producer. But I've got the other kids all sewn up. They can't let anyone else be the Poppycrunch Kid. They put me here to see. To see if I really am the Poppycrunch Kid and if I'm not, then they'll choose someone else. But I'm the one – The Poppycrunch Kid, you said it, you did – when fun happens who's right there, the cereal this kid eats, is the one with the built-in treats, nuts and honey, bite it, munch it, Poppycrunch it.

She could hear them at visiting time.

'Look, Herbert,' said the lady's voice. 'Isn't that the kid who was on the telly? You know, that Poppy-cereal stuff. I'm sure it's her.'

'Don't be silly,' said Herbert. 'She was pretty – full of life. That kid looks half dead to me.'

I'm not, she thought, *I'm full of fun, full of goodness . . . Poppycrunch for me . . .*

The Facts and Fictions of Minna Pratt

PATRICIA MacLACHLAN

Minna paused before the great wooden door of the conservatory and looked up for good luck to where the gargoyles rested, grey and ominous and familiar. Then she pushed open the door and began the walk up the three flights of stairs. There was a lift, but it was self-service, and Minna had nightmares of being stuck there between floors with no one to talk with, nothing to count. Alone with her cello. Minna, of course, would not practise.

> TV ANNOUNCER: *'After three days and two nights of being stranded in a lift, Minna Booth Pratt has emerged, blinking and looking rested.'*
> MINNA: [*Blinking and looking rested.*]
> TV ANNOUNCER: *'A record, ladies and gentlemen!*

> *Seventy-two hours in a lift without*
> *practising!'*
> [*Applause, applause, cheering.*]

Sighing, Minna paused at the first-floor landing to look out the window. Below were McGrew and Emily Parmalee, slumped over like half-filled travel bags, singing. Minna pulled her jacket around her, the chill of the old building numbing her fingers. Far off she heard an oboe playing Ravel, a sound as sad and grey as the building. She walked up the last flight of stairs, slowly, slowly, thinking of yesterday's lesson. It was Bartók, bowing hand for Bartók staccato; swift, short bows, Porch's hand on her elbow, forcing her wrist to do the work. When she got it right, he would smile his Bartók smile: there quickly, then gone. It would be early Haydn today. High third finger, she reminded herself, digging her thumb-nail into the finger, forcing it to remember. After Haydn it would be the Mozart. *The Mozart. K. 157.* The number was etched on her mind, and Minna stopped suddenly, her breath caught in her throat. The Mozart with the terrible andante she couldn't play. The andante her fingers didn't know, *wouldn't* know. And then the wild presto that left her trembling.

Minna shook her head and walked on. Today was chamber group, three of them, with Porch, the fourth, playing the viola part. Called chamber group by all but Porch, who referred to it as 'mass assembled sound'.

Minna would be late. She was always the last one to arrive, no matter what early bus she took. Everyone would be there, Imelda and Porch; Orson Babbitt with his tight black curls and sly smile. Minna pushed the door open with one finger and they were tuning, Porch scuttling sideways like a crab between music stands with an armful of music. Imelda stopped playing and laid her violin on her lap, one foot crossed primly over the other, her black braids slick as snakes.

'It's three thirty-five,' she announced, glancing at the clock. 'And you've got only one sock.'

'That's in case you care,' said Orson, making Minna grin.

Imelda was touched with perfect pitch as well as other annoyances. She pronounced varied facts even when not asked. She could recite the kings of England in order, backwards and forwards, the dates of major gang wars, important comets, what mixtures produced the colour mauve. Imelda: fact-gatherer, data-harvester, bundler of useless news.

'It's W.A. today, Minna,' called Orson from across the room, Orson's name for Wolfgang Amadeus Mozart. Orson played second violin with a sloppy serenity, rolling his eyes and sticking out his tongue, his bowing long and sweeping and beautiful even when out of tune. 'If you must make a mistake,' he had quoted, 'make it a big one.' Was it Heifetz who had said it? Perlman? Zukerman maybe?

'Tune, tune,' said Porch briskly. He turned to Orson. 'And is there a word for today?' Orson was the word person, spilling words out as if they were notes on a staff.

'Rebarbative,' said Orson promptly. 'Causing annoyance or irritation. Mozart's rebarbative music causes me to want to throw up.'

Porch sighed. Orson preferred Schubert.

Suddenly Porch brightened, looking over Minna's head.

'Ah, good. I'd nearly forgotten. There is an addition to our group. A newcomer.'

Everyone looked up. Minna turned.

'This is Lucas Ellerby,' announced Porch, beckoning him in. 'Lucas will play viola with us from now on.'

The boy paused at the doorway. His hair fell over his forehead.

'Imelda and Orson,' introduced Porch. 'Minna Pratt, too.'

Minna smiled. It sounded like the beginning of a nursery rhyme she half remembered:

> *Imelda and Orson and Minna Pratt, too,*
> *Set out in a gleaming bright boat of blue . . .*

'Lucas will play viola next to Minna,' Porch went on. 'I'll play first with Imelda. Trying hard not to be rebarbative.'

Lucas smiled for the first time.

'That bad?' he asked.

Orson looked up quickly. There was a silence while

Lucas unlocked his case and took out his viola and bow. Finally Imelda spoke.

'Have you heard the fact,' she asked, her eyes bright, 'that the Great Wall of China is actually visible from the moon?'

A fact, thought Minna. A mauve fact might follow.

Lucas sat down next to Minna.

'Yes,' he said simply. He smiled a radiant sudden smile at Imelda as he tightened his bow. 'Wonderful, yes? A fine fact.'

Minna watches Lucas's long fingers curl around his viola, one leg stretch out, one slide back to hook over a chair rung. There is a grand silence as they all stare at Lucas. Minna does not fall in love quickly. Most often she eases into love as she eases into a Bach cello suite, slowly and carefully, frowning all the while. She has been in love only once and a half. Once with Norbert with the violent smile who sells eggs from his truck. The half with one of her father's patients, a young man who made her breathless with his winks. When she discovered he also winked at her mother, father, McGrew, and the car, she slipped backwards out of love again.

'Scales first,' said Porch. 'Old, familiar friends, scales. G to start.'

They played scales, staring at nothing, no music needed because Porch was right . . . the scales were old friends.

'Now,' said Porch, 'let's begin with something we

know. Mozart, K. 156. Presto, but not too presto.' He raised his violin. 'An A, everyone.' They played an A, Orson making gagging noises.

Old Back lifted his bow.

The Great Wall of China, thought Minna. A fine fact.

'Ready,' said Porch.

I wish I'd thought of that fine fact. Then Lucas would have smiled at me.

'Here we come, W.A.,' said Orson softly.

'High third finger, Minna,' whispered Porch.

And they play. They begin together and Minna holds her breath. Often they stumble into the music, Porch louder, counting; Imelda scowling and playing too fast; Orson snorting in rhythm. But today is different. They begin on the same note and play together. In tune. Minna looks at Porch and sees that he has noticed the difference, too. Lucas's hand vibrates on the strings. They all hear the strong, rich sound of his vibrato. Lucas peers at Minna and grins. And suddenly Minna realizes that she is smiling. She has never smiled through an entire movement of W. A. Mozart. Ever.

'Splendid, splendid,' said Porch, gathering up the music. Could they be finished already? One entire hour? 'You are a fine addition, Lucas.'

Imelda was smiling. Minna and Orson were smiling. Even Porch smiled.

'Tomorrow,' instructed Porch, 'the K. 157 andante. And the mimeographed variations. Practise! You, too,' Porch said to Minna.

In the coatroom, Lucas locked up his viola. His jacket lay behind the case and he stepped around it carefully, gently picking it up, his hand covering the pocket.

Minna felt she must say something.

'You have,' she began. She cleared her throat. 'You have a wonderful vibrato.'

Dumb, thought Minna with a sinking in her stomach. It was like saying that he had a lovely skin condition. Or both his legs ended nicely below his trousers.

Lucas nodded.

'I got it at music camp,' he said solemnly. He looked apologetic, as if it might have been a mild case of measles, or worse, homesickness.

Lucas put on his jacket, then pulled a frog from the pocket. The frog was quiet and friendly-looking.

'I saved him from the biology lab,' explained Lucas. 'I'm going to put him in the park pond. It's warm enough now.' He looked at Minna. 'Want to come?'

'Yes,' said Minna quickly before he could change his mind.

Together they picked up their cases, Minna hoisting hers on her hip, Lucas's under his arm. In the hallway Lucas pushed the wall button, and it wasn't until the door opened and closed behind them that Minna realized she was in the lift. The walls were grey with things scribbled there. The floor was littered with gum wrappers. There was a half-eaten apple in the corner.

The lift started down, and Minna put out her hand to steady herself.

Lucas looked closely at her.

'Lifts can be scary,' he said in a soft voice.

There was a terrible feeling in Minna's chest. The lift seemed to drop too fast. There was a loud whooshing sound in her ears, and she looked at Lucas to see if he had heard it, too. But he was smiling at his frog. It was then that Minna knew about the sinking feeling and the noise in her head. It was not the lift.

The door opened at the ground floor.

TV ANNOUNCER: *'After three days and two nights, listeners in the vast audience, Melinda Booth Pratt is about to emerge from her lift an accomplished cellist. With a vibrato. Accompanying her is Lucas Ellerby. Food and drink have been lowered to them, along with cello music. And flies for their frog.'*

Outside there was a slight breeze. McGrew and Emily were still sitting on the stone steps.

'This is Lucas,' said Minna. 'My brother, McGrew, and his friend Emily Parmalee, a catcher.'

Lucas smiled. McGrew smiled. *All this smiling.* Emily Parmalee turned one earring around and around in her ear thoughtfully.

'We're going to put Lucas's frog in the park pond before the bus comes,' said Minna.

Behind them the street musicians were beginning to play: a flute on the far corner, Willie, tall and bearded, by the steps playing Vivaldi in the dusk. Willie was Minna's favourite, playing whatever she wanted on his violin, giving her back her money.

They walk down the street, Minna and Lucas with two instruments and a frog between them, McGrew and Emily Parmalee behind, shuffling their feet. The street is crowded but strangely hushed except for the swish sound of cars passing cars. Lucas says nothing. Minna says nothing. Only McGrew breaks the silence.

'Love,' he sings softly in a high thin voice behind Minna.

The Greatest

MICHELLE MAGORIAN

'Boys' group,' said the teacher.

The second group of girls broke away from the centre of the dance studio, their faces flushed, their skin streaming with sweat.

A skinny girl, whose fair hair was scraped up into a bun, smiled at him, and pretended to collapse with exhaustion against the barre.

'Kevin, aren't you a boy any more?' asked the teacher.

'Oh yes!' he exclaimed. 'Sorry.'

He joined the other three boys in the class. They were waiting for him opposite the mirror.

'You've been in a dream today,' she said. 'Now I expect some nice high jumps from you boys, so we'll take it slower. That doesn't mean flat feet. I want to see those feet stretched. First position. And one and two.'

Kevin brought his arms up into first in front of him and out to the side to prepare for the jumps.

He loved the music the pianist chose for them. It made him feel as if he could leap as high and as powerfully as Mikhail Barishnikov. He knew that barre work was important but he liked the exercises in the centre of the studio best, especially when they had to leap.

But today all the spring had gone out of him. A lead weight seemed to pull him down. Bending his knees in a deep *plié* he thrust himself as high as he could into the air.

'I want to see the effort in your legs, not your faces,' remarked the teacher as he was in mid-spring.

They sprang in first position, their feet together, and out into second with their feet apart, then alternated from one to the other, out in, out in, sixteen times in each position, sixteen times for the change-overs.

'Don't collapse when you've finished,' said the teacher. 'Head up. Tummies in. And hold. Right everyone, back into the centre.'

It was the end of class. The girls made wide sweeping curtsies, the boys stepped to each side with the music and bowed.

'Thank you,' said the teacher.

They clapped to show their appreciation, as if they were in an adult class. Kevin knew that was what they did because in the holidays he was sometimes allowed to attend their Beginners' Classes in Ballet, even though he was only ten. He was more advanced than a beginner but at least the classes kept him fit.

Everyone ran to the corner of the studio to pick up their bags. It wasn't wise to leave any belongings in the changing-rooms. Too many things had been stolen from there.

The teacher stood by the door taking money from those who paid per class, or tickets from those whose parents paid for them ten at a time, which was cheaper.

Martin was standing in front of him, pouring out a handful of loose change into the teacher's tin. His father disapproved of boys or men doing ballet so Martin did it in secret and paid for his classes and fares by doing odd jobs. His only pair of dance tights were in ribbons and his dance shoes were so small that they hurt him.

Kevin handed his ticket to the teacher.

'I saw your father earlier on,' she said. 'Whose class is he taking?'

'He's not doing a class. It's an audition.'

'Is that why your head is full of cotton wool today? Worried for him?'

'Not exactly,' he said slowly.

He tugged at Martin's damp T-shirt.

'Dad gave me extra money today. I have to wait for him. Want some orange juice?'

'Yeah,' said Martin eagerly.

'Let's grab a table.'

They ran down the corridor to the canteen area and flung their bags on to chairs.

'I'm bushed,' said Martin.

'Were you sweeping up Mr Grotowsky's shop this morning?'

'Yeah. And I cleaned cars. Dad thinks I'm working this afternoon, too.'

'What if he checks up?'

'He won't. As long as he doesn't see me he doesn't care where I am.'

'Doesn't he wonder why you don't have any money when you go home?'

'No. I tell him I spend it on Wimpy's or fruit machines.'

Although he was only eleven Martin had already decided what he wanted to do with his life. He had it all mapped out. First he'd be a dancer, then a choreographer. His idol was a tall thin black American teacher in the Big Studio. He had performed in and choreographed shows in the West End. Professional dancers and students sweated and slaved for him, arching and stretching, moving in fast rhythms, leaping and spinning. There were black ones there too, like Martin. One day one of those black dancers would be him.

Some of the students were afraid of the teacher but they worked hard to be allowed to get into, and stay in, his classes.

'Get a classical training first,' he had told Martin abruptly when Martin had plucked up enough courage to ask his advice. So that's what Martin was doing.

'What's the audition for?' he asked.

'A musical.'

Kevin put their beakers of orange on to the table.

'So what's the problem? Don't you think he has a chance?'

Kevin shrugged.

'Which one is it?'

'*Guys and Dolls*. He's going up for an acting part. He thinks his best chance of getting work as an actor is if he gets into a musical. He says no one will look at him if they know he's a dancer. He says directors think dancers haven't any brains.'

'I'd like to see them try a class.'

'Yes. That's what Dad says.'

'Is it because you're nervous for him? Is that it?'

'No. We had a row this morning. We just ended up shouting at one another. We didn't talk to each other all the way here. Even in the changing-room.'

'What was the row about?'

'About him auditioning for this job. I don't want him to get it.'

'Why? He's been going to enough voice classes.'

'Yes, I know,' he mumbled.

For the last year his father had been doing voice exercises every morning, taking singing lessons, working on scenes from plays at the Actors' Centre, practising audition speeches and songs, and reading plays.

'I didn't think he'd have to go away, though. This theatre's a repertory theatre and it's miles away. I'd only see him at the weekend. And even then it'd probably only be Sundays. And if he got it he'd start rehearsing two weeks after I start school.'

'So? You've been there before. Not like me. I start at the Comprehensive in a week's time. It'll be back to Saturday classes only.' He swallowed the last dregs of his orange juice.

'Want another? Dad said it was OK.'

'Yeah. I'll go and get them.'

Kevin handed him the money and pulled on his track-suit top over his T-shirt even though he was still boiling from the class.

He couldn't imagine his father being an actor. But his father had explained that he couldn't be a dancer all his life, that choreographers would eventually turn him down for younger dancers and, in fact, had already done so a couple of times. He had to decide which direction he wanted to go in before that started to become a habit.

For the last two years, since Kevin's mother had died, his father had only accepted work in cabaret in London, or bit parts in films, or had given dance classes. Otherwise he had been on the dole. Kevin was used to him being around now.

When his mother was alive and his parents were touring with a dance company, Kevin used to stay with a friend of the family. Dad said it would be like old times staying with her again. Kevin didn't want it to be like old times. He wanted things to stay just as they were.

He pulled on his track-suit trousers, dumped his holdall on his chair and waved to Martin.

'I'll be back in a minute,' he yelled.

He ran down the two flights of stairs which led to the entrance hall, past two of the studios there and downstairs to the basement where the changing-rooms and other studios were.

Outside the studio where the audition was taking place stood a crowd of people peering in at the windows. They were blocking the corridor so that dancers going to and from the changing-room had to keep pushing their way through with an urgent, 'Excuse me!'

The door to the studio opened and six disappointed men came out. Kevin's father wasn't among them.

Kevin squeezed in between two people by one of the windows and peered in.

Inside the steamed-up studio a group of men of every age, height and shape were listening to a woman director. A man was sitting at a piano.

The director was smiling and waving her arms about.

'Here. Squeeze in here,' said a dancer in a red leo-tard. 'You can see better. They're auditioning for *Guys and Dolls*. It's the men's turn today.'

Kevin didn't let on that he knew.

'She's really putting them through it,' said the dancer. 'First they have to sing on their own and the MD, that's the man at the piano, decides who's going to stay. Then they have to learn a song together.'

'What's the song?' asked Kevin.

'"Luck Be a Lady Tonight." Know it?'

Kevin nodded.

Know it? As soon as his father had heard he had been given the audition every song from *Guys and Dolls* had been played from breakfast to bedtime.

'Then they have to do an improvisation. The director chooses who to keep out of that lot and then the choreographer teaches them a dance routine.'

The dancing would be kid's stuff for his father, thought Kevin. He wiped the glass. His father was standing listening. So, he'd passed two singing tests. Now it was the acting.

The director was obviously explaining what the scene was about. She was pointing to individual men.

'She's telling them about the characters,' said the dancer.

Kevin felt angry. How could his father go through with it when he knew that Kevin didn't want him to go away? He observed his father's face, watched him grip his arms in front of himself and then quickly drop them and let out a breath.

'Excuse me!' he said fiercely, and he pushed himself out of the crowd and along the corridor to the stairs. And then he stopped. He remembered the look on his father's face and realized it was one of anxiety. It astounded him. He had seen his father upset before, but never scared. Why would he be scared? He was a brilliant dancer. But now, of course, he also needed to be a good actor. He was trying something new in front of actors who had been doing it for years and some of those actors were younger than him. That took guts, as Martin would say.

Kevin hadn't given a thought to how nervous his father might have been feeling. He knew how badly he missed the theatre. To start a new career when you were as old as him must be hard; harder too when he knew that Kevin hoped he would fail.

He turned and ran back down the corridor, ducked his head and pushed his way back into the crowd to where the dancer in the red leotard was standing. He wasn't too late. They hadn't started the improvisation yet. He stared through the glass willing his father to look at him.

The director stopped talking. The men began to move, their heads down in concentration as she backed away.

Please look this way, thought Kevin.

And then he did. He frowned and gazed sadly at him.

Kevin raised his thumb and mouthed, 'Good luck!'

At that his father's face burst into a smile.

'Thanks,' he mouthed back and he winked.

Kevin gave a wave and backed away through the crowd and along the corridor.

It was going to be all right, he thought. If his father did get the acting job he knew he'd be taken backstage and he'd meet lots of new people, and at least he wouldn't be touring so he could stay with him sometimes. And Martin could come too. And Dad would be happy again.

Martin wasn't at the table. Their bags were still there with the two plastic beakers of orange juice.

Kevin knew where to find him. He walked to the corridor. Martin was gazing with admiration through one of the windows into the Big Studio. His idol was giving a class to the professional dancers.

He grinned when he saw Kevin.

'Guess what!' he squeaked. 'I was by the door when he went in and he noticed me. And he spoke to me. He looked at my shoes and he said I ought to swap them for bigger ones at Lost Property and then, you know what he said? He said, "Say I sent you!"'

He turned back to watching the class and sighed.

'Isn't he the greatest?'

'Yes,' agreed Kevin, and he thought of his father. 'Yes, he's the greatest.'

The Enchanted Castle

E. NESBIT

There never was such a feast provided by any French governess since French governesses began. There were jokes and stories and laughter. Jimmy showed all those tricks with forks and corks and matches and apples which are so deservedly popular. Mademoiselle told them stories of her own school-days when she was 'a quiet little girl with two tight tresses – so,' and when they could not understand the tresses, called for paper and pencil and drew the loveliest little picture of herself when she was a child with two short fat pigtails sticking out from her head like knitting-needles from a ball of dark worsted. Then she drew pictures of everything they asked for, till Mabel pulled Gerald's jacket and whispered: 'The acting!'

'Draw us the front of a theatre,' said Gerald tactfully, 'a French theatre.'

'They are the same thing as the English theatres,' Mademoiselle told him.

'Do you like acting – the theatre, I mean?'

'But yes – I love it.'

'All right,' said Gerald briefly. 'We'll act a play for you – now – this afternoon if you like.'

'Eliza will be washing up,' Cathy whispered, 'and she was promised to see it.'

'Or this evening,' said Gerald; 'and please, Mademoiselle, may Eliza come in and look on?'

'But certainly,' said Mademoiselle; 'amuse yourselves well, my children.'

'But it's *you*,' said Mabel suddenly, 'that we want to amuse. Because we love you very much – don't we, all of you?'

'Yes,' the chorus came unhesitatingly. Though the others would never have thought of saying such a thing on their own account. Yet, as Mabel said it, they found to their surprise that it was true.

'Tiens!' said Mademoiselle, 'You love the old French governess? Impossible.' And she spoke rather indistinctly.

'You're not old,' said Mabel; 'at least not so very,' she added brightly, 'and you're as lovely as a Princess.'

'Go then, flatteress!' said Mademoiselle, laughing; and Mabel went. The others were already half-way up the stairs.

Mademoiselle sat in the drawing-room as usual, and it was a good thing that she was not engaged in serious study, for it seemed that the door opened and shut almost ceaselessly all throughout the afternoon. Might they have the embroidered antimacassars and the sofa cushions? Might they have the clothes-line out of the wash-house? Eliza said they mightn't, but might they? Might they have the sheepskin hearth-rugs? Might they have tea in the garden, because they had almost got the stage ready in the dining-room, and Eliza wanted to set tea? Could Mademoiselle lend them any coloured clothes — scarves or dressing-gowns, or anything bright? Yes, Mademoiselle could, and did — silk things, surprisingly lovely for a governess to have. Had Mademoiselle any rouge? They had always heard that French ladies — No, Mademoiselle hadn't — and to judge by the colour of her face, Mademoiselle didn't need it. Did Mademoiselle think the chemist sold rouge — or had she any false hair to spare? At this challenge Mademoiselle's pale fingers pulled out a dozen hairpins, and down came the love-liest blue-black hair, hanging to her knees in straight, heavy lines.

'No, you terrible infants,' she cried. 'I have not the false hair, nor the rouge. And my teeth — you want them also, without doubt?'

She showed them in a laugh.

'I *said* you were a Princess,' said Mabel, 'and now I know. You're Rapunzel. Do always wear your hair like that! May we have the peacock fans, please, off the mantelpiece, and the things that loop back the curtains, and all the handkerchiefs you've got?'

Mademoiselle denied them nothing. They had the fans and the handkerchiefs and some large sheets of expensive drawing-paper out of the school cupboard, and Mademoiselle's best sable paintbrush and her paintbox.

'Who would have thought,' murmured Gerald, pensively sucking the brush and gazing at the paper mask he had just painted, 'that she was such a brick in disguise? I wonder why crimson lake always tastes just like Liebig's Extract.'

Everything was pleasant that day somehow. There are some days like that, you know, when everything goes well from the very beginning; all the things you want are in their places, nobody misunderstands you, and all that you do turns out admirably. How different from those other days which we all know too well, when your shoe-lace breaks, your comb is mislaid, your brush spins on its back on the floor and lands under the bed where you can't get at it – you drop the soap, your buttons come off, an eyelash gets into your eye, you have used your last clean handkerchief, your collar is frayed at the edge and cuts your neck, and at the very last moment your suspender breaks, and there is no string. On such a day as this you are naturally late for breakfast, and everyone thinks you did it on purpose. And the day goes on and on, getting worse and worse – you mislay your exercise book, you drop your arithmetic in the mud, your pencil breaks, and when you open your knife to sharpen the pencil you split your nail. On such a day you jam your thumb in doors, and muddle the messages you are sent on by grown-ups. You upset your tea, and your bread and butter won't hold together for a moment. And when at last you get to bed – usually in disgrace – it is no comfort at all to you to know that not a single bit of it is your own fault.

This day was not one of those days, as you will have noticed. Even the tea in the garden – there was a bricked bit by a rockery that made a steady floor for the tea-table – was most delightful, though the thoughts of four out of the five were busy with the coming play, and the fifth had thoughts of her own that had nothing to do with tea or acting.

Then there was an interval of slamming doors, interesting silences, feet that flew up and down stairs.

It was still good daylight when the dinner-bell rang – the signal had been agreed upon at tea-time, and carefully explained to Eliza. Mademoiselle laid down her book and passed out of the sunset-yellowed hall into the faint yellow gaslight of the dining-room. The giggling Eliza held the door open before her, and followed her in. The shutters had been closed – streaks of daylight showed above and below them. The green-and-black table-cloths of the school dining-tables were supported on the clothes-line from the backyard. The line sagged in a graceful curve, but it answered its purpose of supporting the curtains which concealed that part of the room which was the stage.

Rows of chairs had been placed across the other end of the room – all the chairs in the house, as it seemed – and Mademoiselle started violently when she saw that fully half a dozen of these chairs were occupied. And by the queerest people, too – an old woman with a poke-bonnet tied under her chin with a red handkerchief, a lady in a large straw hat wreathed in flowers and the oddest hands that stuck out over the chair in front of her, several men with strange, clumsy figures, and all with hats on.

'But,' whispered Mademoiselle, through the chinks of the table-cloths, 'you have then invited other friends? You should have asked me, my children.'

Laughter and something like a 'hurrah' answered her from behind the folds of the curtaining table-cloths.

'All right, Mademoiselle Rapunzel,' cried Mabel; 'turn the gas up. It's only part of the entertainment.'

Eliza, still giggling, pushed through the lines of chairs, knocking off the hat of one of the visitors as she did so, and turned up the three incandescent burners.

Mademoiselle looked at the figure seated nearest to her, stooped to look more closely, half laughed, quite screamed, and sat down suddenly.

'Oh!' she cried, 'they are not alive!'

Eliza, with a much louder scream, had found out the same thing and announced it differently. 'They ain't got no insides,' said she. The seven members of the audience seated among the wilderness of chairs had, indeed, no insides to speak of. Their bodies were bolsters and rolled-up blankets, their spines were broom-handles, and their arm and leg bones were hockey sticks and umbrellas. Their shoulders were the wooden cross-pieces that Mademoiselle used for keeping her jackets in shape; their hands were gloves stuffed out with handkerchiefs; and their faces were the paper masks painted in the afternoon by the untutored brush of Gerald, tied on to the round heads made of the ends of stuffed bolster-cases. The faces were really rather dreadful. Gerald had done his best, but even after his best had been done you would hardly have known they were faces, some of them, if they hadn't been in the positions which faces usually occupy, between the collar and the hat. Their eyebrows were furious with lamp-black frowns – their eyes the size, and almost the shape, of five-shilling pieces, and on their lips and cheeks had been spent much crimson lake and nearly the whole of a half-pan of vermilion.

'You have made yourself an auditors, yes? Bravo!' cried Mademoiselle, recovering herself and beginning to clap. And to the sound of that clapping the curtain went up – or, rather, apart. A voice said, in a breathless, choked way, 'Beauty and the Beast,' and the stage was revealed.

It was a real stage too – the dining-tables pushed close together and covered with pink-and-white counterpanes. It was a little unsteady and creaky to walk on, but very imposing to look at. The scene was simple, but convincing. A big sheet of cardboard, bent square, with slits cut in it and a candle behind, represented, quite transparently, the domestic hearth;

a round hat-tin of Eliza's, supported on a stool with a night-light under it, could not have been mistaken, save by wilful malice, for anything but a copper. A waste-paper basket with two or three school dusters and an overcoat in it, and a pair of blue pyjamas over the back of a chair, put the finishing touch to the scene. It did not need the announcement from the wings, 'The laundry at Beauty's home.' It was so plainly a laundry and nothing else.

In the wings: 'They look just like a real audience, don't they?' whispered Mabel. 'Go on, Jimmy – don't forget the Merchant has to be pompous and use long words.'

Jimmy, enlarged by pillows under Gerald's best overcoat, which had been intentionally bought with a view to his probable growth during the two years which it was intended to last him, a Turkish towel turban on his head and an open umbrella over it, opened the first act in a simple and swift soliloquy:

'I am the most unlucky merchant that ever was. I was once the richest merchant in Baghdad, but I lost all my ships, and now I live in a poor house that is all to bits; you can see how the rain comes through the roof, and my daughters take in washing. And –'

The pause might have seemed long, but Gerald rustled in, elegant in Mademoiselle's pink dressing-gown and the character of the eldest daughter.

'A nice drying day,' he minced. 'Pa dear, put the umbrella the other way up. It'll save us going out in the rain to fetch water. Come on, sisters, dear father's got us a new wash-tub. Here's luxury!'

Round the umbrella, now held the wrong way up, the three sisters knelt and washed imaginary linen. Kathleen wore a violet skirt of Eliza's, a blue blouse of her own, and a cap of knotted handkerchiefs. A white night-dress girt with a white apron and two red carnations in Mabel's black hair left no doubt as to which of the three was Beauty.

The scene went very well. The final dance with waving towels was all that there is of charming, Mademoiselle said; and Eliza was so much amused that, as she said, she got quite a nasty stitch along of laughing so hearty.

You know pretty well what Beauty and the Beast would be like acted by four children who had spent the afternoon in arranging their costumes and so had left no time for rehearsing what they had to say. Yet it delighted them, and it charmed their audience. And what more can any play do, even Shakespeare's? Mabel, in her Princess clothes, was a resplendent Beauty; and Gerald a Beast who wore the drawing-room hearthrugs with an air of indescribable distinction. If Jimmy was not a talkative merchant, he made it up with a stoutness practically unlimited, and Kathleen surprised and delighted even herself by the quickness with which she changed from one to the other of the minor characters – fairies, servants, and messengers. It was at the end of the second act that Mabel, whose costume, having reached the height of elegance, could not be bettered and therefore did not need to be changed, said to Gerald, sweltering under the weighty magnificence of his beast-skin:

'I say, you might let us have the ring back.'

'I'm going to,' said Gerald, who had quite forgotten it. 'I'll give it you in the next scene. Only don't lose it, or go putting it on. You might go out all together and never be seen again, or you might get seven times as visible as anyone else, so that all the rest of us would look like shadows beside you, you'd be so thick, or –'

'Ready!' said Kathleen, bustling in, once more a wicked sister.

Gerald managed to get his hand into his pocket under his hearthrug, and when he rolled his eyes in agonies of sentiment, and said, 'Farewell, dear Beauty! Return quickly, for if you remain long absent from your faithful beast he will assuredly perish,' he pressed a ring into her hand and added: 'This is a magic ring that will give you anything you wish. When you desire to return to your own disinterested beast, put on the ring and utter your wish. Instantly you will be by my side.'

Beauty-Mabel took the ring, and it was *the* ring.

The curtains closed to warm applause from two pairs of hands.

The next scene went splendidly. The sisters were almost *too* natural in their disagreeableness, and Beauty's annoyance when they splashed her Princess's dress with real soap and water was considered a miracle of good acting. Even the merchant rose to something more than mere pillows, and the curtain fell on his pathetic assurance that in the absence of his dear

Beauty he was wasting away to a shadow. And again two pairs of hands applauded.

'Here, Mabel, catch hold,' Gerald appealed from under the weight of a towel-horse, the tea-urn, the tea-tray, and the green baize apron of the boot boy, which together with four red geraniums from the landing, the pampas-grass from the drawing-room fireplace, and the India rubber plants from the drawing-room window were to represent the fountains and garden of the last act. The applause had died away.

'I wish,' said Mabel, taking on herself the weight of the tea-urn, 'I wish those creatures we made were alive. We should get something like applause then.'

'I'm jolly glad they aren't,' said Gerald, arranging the baize and the towel-horse. 'Brutes! It makes me feel quite silly when I catch their paper eyes.'

The curtains were drawn back. There lay the hearthrug-coated beast, in flat abandonment among the tropic beauties of the garden, the pampas-grass shrubbery, the India rubber plant bushes, the geranium trees and the urn fountain. Beauty was ready to make her great entry in all the thrilling splendour of despair. And then suddenly it all happened.

Mademoiselle began it: she applauded the garden scene – with hurried little clappings of her quick French hands. Eliza's fat red palms followed heavily, and then – someone else was clapping, six or seven people, and their clapping made a dull padded sound. Nine faces instead of two were turned towards the stage, and seven out of the nine were painted, pointed paper faces. And every hand and every face was alive. The applause grew louder as Mabel glided forward, and as she paused and looked at the audience her unstudied pose of horror and amazement drew forth applause louder still; but it was not loud enough to drown the shrieks of Mademoiselle and Eliza as they rushed from the room, knocking chairs over and crushing each other in the doorway. Two distant doors banged, Mademoiselle's door and Eliza's door.

'Curtain! Curtain! Quick!' cried Beauty-Mabel, in a voice that wasn't Mabel's or the Beauty's. 'Jerry – those things *have* come alive. Oh, whatever *shall* we do?'

Gerald in his hearthrugs leaped to his feet. Again that flat padded applause marked the swish of cloths on clothes-line as Jimmy and Kathleen drew the curtains.

'What's up?' they asked as they drew.

'You've done it this time!' said Gerald to the pink, perspiring Mabel. 'Oh, bother these strings!'

'Can't you burst them? *I've* done it?' retorted Mabel. 'I like that!'

'More than I do,' said Gerald.

'Oh, it's all right,' said Mabel, 'Come on. We must go and pull the things to pieces – then they *can't* go on being alive.'

'It's your fault, anyhow,' said Gerald with every possible absence of gallantry. 'Don't you see? It's turned into a wishing ring. I *knew* something different was going to happen. Get my knife out of my pocket

– this string's in a knot. Jimmy, Cathy, those Ugly-Wuglies have come alive – because Mabel wished it. Cut out and pull them to pieces.'

Jimmy and Cathy peeped through the curtain and recoiled with white faces and staring eyes. 'Not me!' was the brief rejoinder of Jimmy. Cathy said, 'Not much!' And she meant it, anyone could see that.

And now, as Gerald, almost free of the hearthrugs, broke his thumb-nail on the stiffest blade of his knife, a thick rustling and a sharp, heavy stumping sounded beyond the curtain.

'They're going out!' screamed Kathleen – '*walking* out – on their umbrella and broomstick legs. You can't stop them, Jerry, they're too awful!'

'Everybody in the town'll be insane by tomorrow night if we *don't* stop them,' cried Gerald. 'Here, give me the ring – I'll unwish them.'

He caught the ring from the unresisting Mabel, cried, 'I wish the Uglies *weren't* alive,' and tore through the door. He saw, in fancy, Mabel's wish undone, and the empty hall strewed with limp bolsters, hats, umbrellas, coats and gloves, prone abject properties from which the brief life had gone out for ever. But the hall was crowded with live things, strange things – all horribly short as broomsticks and umbrellas are short. A limp hand gesticulated. A pointed white face with red cheeks looked up at him, and wide red lips said something, he could not tell what. The voice reminded him of the old beggar down by the bridge who had no roof to his mouth.

These creatures had no roofs to their mouths, of course
– they had no –

'Aa oo ré o me me oo a oo ho el?' said the voice
again. And it had said it four times before Gerald
could collect himself sufficiently to understand that
this horror – alive, and most likely quite uncontrol-
lable – was saying, with a dreadful calm, polite persist-
ence:

'Can you recommend me to a good hotel?'

She Shall Have Music

KITTY BARNE

They were having eggs for tea in honour of Karen's festival. Her class was to be heard at seven o'clock. They were all going to support her, even Biddy, leaving Benjie to take care of the house, which he did exceedingly well, barking like a kennelful of dogs if he heard a sound.

'You must be sure to see that your bedroom doors are shut,' said Mrs Forrest, pouring out for Ralph and Meg; the others had not yet appeared. 'You know what Benjie is.'

Sleeping on beds was Benjie's secret vice. When left alone in the house he went from room to room having forty winks on each in turn like the child in *The Three Bears*.

'All right, mum. I'll hop round last thing,' said Ralph. 'Anyhow, there's heaps of time.'

'I can't think what's happened to Judy,' said Mrs Forrest. 'She can't be helping Karen to dress all this time.'

'Oh, can't she!' said Meg, significantly. 'Have you seen it?'

Ralph looked up from his egg.

'Seen what?'

'The dress.'

'What's it like?'

'Black velvet.'

'Cripes! With bugles?'

'Don't be silly,' said Mrs Forrest. 'It's a very nice dress. Quite simple, even if it is black. It was very kind of Rosalba to give it to her.'

'Oh, well, if it's *given* . . .' said Ralph, reassured. 'Anyway, it'll do for mourning.'

'I don't know that it's any worse than the red one,' said Meg. 'But have you seen her hair?'

'No, what's she done to it? Dyed it?'

'You're being ridiculous, both of you,' said their mother, anxiously however, for she had not seen Karen since lunch. She had darted out directly she had swallowed her last mouthful, saying Rosalba wanted her but she didn't know what for, and danced in only ten minutes before tea with the cardboard box containing her new dress under her arm.

'Of course they haven't done anything to her hair. She has probably been having it washed – shampooed. Most extravagant of Rosalba.'

'Washed!' Meg snorted. 'It's waved.'

'Not *permed*!' For a moment Mrs Forrest was shaken out of her usual calm. Then she recovered herself. Rosalba was a person of taste. Also there had been no time for a long process like that. Also, of course, she would never dream of doing such a lasting affair without asking leave.

'No, of course not,' she answered herself. 'Don't go putting ideas into my head. I expect she has just had it properly done for once and it's taken a wave.'

'You don't catch Karen's hair taking anything like that. It's dead straight. But it's been water-waved, whatever that is. Judy thinks it's lovely. She's all over it, and the dress too.'

Meg was nothing if not fair-minded. How Judy could encourage this kind of thing she could not imagine. She herself would have taken the wettest, hardest brush she could find and got the waves out as quick as possible. But then nothing would have induced her to wear the black velvet dress either, whereas Judy was green with envy – or so she said.

'Oh well,' said Mrs Forrest, 'I dare say it's a good thing to look as nice as you can if you play the piano. Anyway, Karen had nothing to wear. She had grown out of everything.'

The door opened and Judy ushered Karen in, like a showman announcing a performing animal.

'Miss Karen Forrest.'

Rosalba had dressed her in new things from top to toe. She had new shoes, a new petticoat under the velvet dress; every single thing she wore was new, down to her vest, which was blue for luck.

Her hair, instead of being brushed back from her bumpy forehead in its usual way, was waved as much

59

as its length would allow and surmounted by a huge bow.

'Darling! . . .' breathed her mother, taken aback. Karen looked, somehow, so unlike herself.

'Isn't she simply grand?' said Judy, with a showman's pride.

'Did the hairdresser give you the bow for your hair, darling?'

'No, I did that,' said Judy. 'Don't you like it?'

'It's fearful,' said Meg solemnly. 'Simply fearful.'

Karen looked at them all, beaming. She had not looked in the glass and she had no idea there was anything unusual about her. All she knew was that she had had a wonderful day with darling Rosalba, being given presents as if it were Christmas. She had never known anything like it.

Judy looked doubtfully at her handiwork.

'What do you think, Ralph?'

'It's a bit off, that bow,' he said with a judicial air.

'Yes, I agree,' said his mother. 'Let's take it away.'

The bow was untied and Karen's hair fell into its ordinary position.

'Oh, all right,' said Judy, and attacked her egg philosophically. 'Have it your own way. I don't believe you've got a scrap of taste, any of you.'

Karen was glad to be rid of the bow. It was inclined to flap about when she moved her head. Anyway, it didn't matter. Nothing mattered. She had played all the six pieces to old Mrs Mersey-White that afternoon, on the Steinway with the lid open, and the old lady said it was beautiful and that she was sure to get the prize with all the help Rosalba was giving her. Now all she was longing for was seven o'clock, time to begin.

'I've just heard from Aunt Anne. She's coming up from Sharpset to hear you, Karen. She rang up Mr Bell to say so.' Mr Bell was the grocer next door who good-naturedly took telephone messages for them.

'Oh, how lovely!' cried Karen. That Aunt Anne should be there was just the lovely last golden straw. Aunt Anne would be pleased, she knew. She had got that left hand much better. She still hoped that the choice would not fall on the Bach, anything rather than that; still, if it did she could manage. Derry's advice had been good. Derry *knew* all right.

She gave Benjie a goodbye kiss, and he gave her two or three thumps with his tail for good luck. The soup for their supper was left in the saucepan ready to hot up the moment they came in. Then she re-membered she had no handkerchief and she had to tear upstairs for it. After that she was ready; she put on the same fur gloves that Rosalba had lent her for the Women's Institute concert, Ralph seized the blue case with her music, and they were off.

They found Rosalba, in a fur coat and no hat, frown-ing in the doorway of the hall where the festival was being held. She had kept places for them, she said, and someone had come who she thought might be their

Aunt Anne. Whoever it was she was sitting there waiting for them. They were none too early, and had Karen kept her hands warm, and was she sure she hadn't forgotten any of her music? Would she look in her case and see? Karen looked and there it all was, safe and sound, but, as she said, it didn't matter anyway because she was playing it all by heart.

They went into the hall and sat in a long row: Rosalba in the gangway seat, Mrs Forrest next, then Ralph, Judy, Meg, and Aunt Anne – six of them. It was a long time before Rosalba settled down. She had four programmes for them, already marked with a large cross against Karen's name and number. The competitors were all given numbers, chosen by lot like the two pieces. She was to listen for her number and when it was called out that meant she had to go and play on the enormous piano on the platform. She must be sure to hear it.

'I see,' said Mrs Forrest, when Rosalba had explained all this. 'We'll all listen. You may be sure we won't let her miss it.'

'And Karen must sit at the end of the row so that she can get out quickly,' said Rosalba urgently.

'I don't think that matters,' came from Aunt Anne, in a large calm voice. 'She can sit here by me and slip past these people very easily.' There were three people between her and the end of the row.

'Oh, very well,' said Rosalba, worriedly, 'if you really think so.'

'I really do,' said Aunt Anne with her bland smile, and Karen sat down beside her.

'Here, Karen, hang on to your music.'

Ralph passed the blue case down the line to her.

'Don't hold that heavy case,' said Rosalba. 'Don't touch it, darling. It'll tire your wrist. *Never* hold anything.'

'Never? That's a little difficult, isn't it?' Aunt Anne gave a sniff and pulled out a bag of pear-drops. 'With Mrs Bent's love. Have one, and remember, Karen, whatever you do, don't *fuss*.'

'I'm not fussing,' said Karen, and took a pear-drop. What was the matter with Rosalba? It was like the audition all over again.

'No, I know you're not,' said Aunt Anne. 'Why should you? Nothing on earth to fuss about. Let's see where you come. Where's your number?'

'Page fourteen,' said Rosalba, seizing the programme out of Aunt Anne's hand. 'There it is. Her number is seven. It's a lucky number – makes such a difference.'

A man came to the edge of the platform.

'Ssh, he's going to announce the draw. Which piece, you know.'

Karen clasped her hands together. She could hardly believe her ears. The lot had fallen on the Mendelssohn in the first group and the Chopin waltz in the second – the two things she loved best. 'Oh, hooray, hooray, hooray,' she breathed into Aunt Anne's ear.

'Number one,' called the man.

'They're beginning,' gasped Rosalba; and with a whispered 'Good luck' to Karen she rushed to her place at the end of the row.

The adjudicator was sitting at a table covered with papers in the gangway, half-way down the hall. He had grey hair and bushy eyebrows; that much Karen had seen when he stood up to beckon to someone. 'Right,' he said, in a nice ordinary sort of voice, and nodded to the man on the platform.

The first three candidates were girls of nearly sixteen. To Karen they seemed very nearly grown up. The first one looked very shy and she played the Mendelssohn in a shy way, though she made no mistakes. She seemed rather afraid of the Chopin too. Everyone clapped her when she had done but she only smiled thankfully as if she were glad to get it over. The next two were good, Karen thought; but after them came a boy of twelve or so with a round dark head and a long nose. He dashed into the waltz, taking it much faster than the other three and playing it much louder. He fairly took Karen's breath away and at first she thought him wonderful. Then he began to lose his way; he repeated a bar and took a wrong turning that led him back to the very beginning of the piece. Then he floundered and skipped a bit, and all he could do was to play faster and faster. Karen seized Aunt Anne by the hand. 'He's wrong. Oh, *poor* boy, he's gone wrong.' She longed to help him.

'Start again,' said the adjudicator in a calm voice. He gave a worried grin and began again, this time playing it beautifully from beginning to end.

'There,' said Aunt Anne. 'You see what happens if you lose your head. He could play it perfectly –

though he had no business to go galloping through it at that pace.'

They clapped him all the more because he had broken down, and the next one began. She was good, too; no wrong notes, no hesitations. They were all good, in fact, but, Karen said to herself, Rosalba would not think much of them. She would say they were dull. She would use her favourite word, which Karen never understood, and say they had no 'personality'. What exactly that was Karen did not know, but she could see for herself that these people were very unlike Rosalba. They sat so still; they none of them swayed to the music as she did; they none of them tried the piano over with an arpeggio. None of them, in fact, did any of the extra things she did. Karen felt sorry for them, not having had the luck to be taught by darling Rosalba. Number five had a mop of hair as curly as Judy's and the audience applauded her more than any one. She was better; she smiled and bowed in rather more Rosalba's way. Number six looked older than any of them. She was a big heavy girl who sat down to the piano very quietly and played in a way of her own. 'I like her,' thought Karen. 'I'd like her to go on and on.' She was the first one to make the piano sing. Suddenly its tone was beautiful, and Karen was reminded of Miriam Hals. The audience liked her too; they clapped her quite as much as the curly-headed one, though she took very little notice of them. An unsmiling, interesting sort of girl.

'Number seven,' called the man from the platform, and Ralph leant forward to remind Karen that seven was her number. She mustn't be a little cuckoo and forget to go up there and play. He felt suddenly responsible for her. Supposing she broke down like that ass of a boy! How awful that would be! But no, she seemed all right. She hopped up as if she was quite pleased to go, and sat down at the piano. She had a handkerchief – thank goodness it was a clean one – with which she seemed to be rubbing her hands like a fly cleaning its back legs. Having done that she put it on the side of the piano and played a perky little bit before getting off on her piece. The handkerchief business seemed to be an extra; no one else had done it, anyway. The piece itself was going pretty well. Ralph was getting to know it having heard it six times, and as far as he could see she was getting down to it all right; very like the others to listen to, of course, but not at all like them to look at. Quite extraordinarily unlike, in fact. She was moving all the time; sometimes her head came down nearly to her hands, for all the world as if she was going into a football scrum. Was that the thing to do? Perhaps it was. People had all sorts of tricks when they were bowling and that was considered rather good. Characteristic action, they called it. The audience applauded after the Mendelssohn and Karen got up and bowed, or rather gave the little curtsey that Rosalba had taught her, and sat down again. No one else had done that and Ralph felt slightly uncomfortable. Someone ought to tell the kid that it looked rather too like asking people to clap. She wouldn't think of it herself, of course, but if every one else sat tight she ought to. And the playing of the little twiddly bits before beginning properly, wasn't that perhaps showing off? He must find out. It was bad luck on the kid to let her do it if it wasn't quite good form. He looked at Rosalba. She was leaning forward, gazing at Karen with what Ralph thought a silly expression, clapping wildly. He felt uncomfortable again. It might be all right for music but that wasn't the way you taught anything else. Did Rosalba know as much as she let on? Was she any good? Look at the way she had fussed at the door. Enough to put any one off, let alone a kid only just eleven. The second piece began. No fear of Karen breaking down, she was fairly walking into it and grinning like anything. But what a queer action she had – that way of pawing the air like a dog swimming. It was over and the audience was clapping and laughing. They seemed to be amused. Why? It wasn't supposed to be funny, was it? Perhaps it was only because she was a bit younger. Ralph clapped as loud as he could. Jolly good effort. Good kid. He decided to give her half a crown for her piano money.

'Number eight,' called the man from the platform. Karen's moment was over.

She sat down, panting a little, at the end of a row behind the others. It had been glorious, like running a race, like learning to dive; she had never done anything half so exciting in her life. She would wait there till the adjudicator told them who were the recalled candidates. He had said he would announce that after the last player. They were to play again that evening at nine o'clock. She wondered how many would be recalled. Not the boy, certainly, and not the first girl. She herself might have just a chance. At all events she had never played so well in her life. She had re-membered to smile when she was playing the waltz. She had remembered almost everything. Rosalba had leant forward and caught her eye and clapped, so she was pleased and that was what mattered most. Darling Rosalba.

Number nine finished and the adjudicator made his way on to the platform. He had had a long day, listening and listening, his critical faculties full stretch all the time. His grey hair was on end and his grey eyebrows bushier than ever as he stood there, a sheaf of papers in his hand. However, he had something interesting and often nice to say about everybody. Number one must have a bit more confidence; she had a nice touch and a good left hand, but her playing had no life in it. The boy, he said, let the music run away with him. He must learn control and try again next year. The big girl had the best tone he had heard yet from any one in the festival, and so on.

Then he came to number seven.

'This little girl –' he said in his pleasant voice, shak-ing his shaggy head, 'this little girl is going to get a bad shock, I'm afraid. I can't give any marks at all to a player with such terrible style. She must get rid of all the fuss, all the frills and furbelows, all these dreadful airs and graces, and let the music she undoubtedly . . .'

Karen lost his voice, deafened by a noise like a thousand kettles singing in her ears. Her heart beat as if she had had a sudden dreadful fright. An enormous blush spread over her from her heels to her head. He was talking about her – Karen – and what on earth was he saying? Something about simplicity and affectation – long words she knew nothing about. Couldn't she get away? She was at the end of a row. Her one idea was to escape from this awful voice from the platform that said things about her she could not understand. She wasn't crying yet but in another minute she would be, a sob was half choking her.

She got up quietly, slipped down the side gangway, through the swing-doors, and out into the street. Then she took to her heels and ran and ran.

A Swarm in May

WILLIAM MAYNE

John Owen stood in a narrow street full of narrow shadows: they stood in the corners of every beamed and overhanging house-front. There was light and dark up to the saw-like stepped edge of each tiled gable, and beyond that a blue night sky with very small shivering stars.

In the street there was no one but John Owen himself. On the wall in front of him there was bright light on white stone and on a small black door. The door was the small postern in the gateway; beside it there was the big gate you could take a car through. Both gates were closed now, because it was after nine o'clock: if you wanted to go in, you rang the bell. John Owen had already done that, but he had to wait until the watchman, Turle, came with the key.

'Very old Turtle,' said John Owen. 'Stop hibernating.' But he did not mind the last few moments of holiday being stretched out longer; though there was

a wind lurking in the shadows and coming out pinch-
ingly against his ankles. The light against the pale
stone of the gateway was bright and splendid: it
looked like sunlight but it struck cold. Even the coats
of arms, looking down from their row of shields
above the archway in red and blue, black and gold,
were not warming on a May night.

Turle's footsteps sounded inside the gate. The key
turned and the lock jumped back: a bold sound in an
empty street.

'What do you want?' said Turle, when he saw only
a boy standing outside.

'Choir School,' said John Owen.

'What's your name?' said Turle.

'Owen.'

'Bit late,' said Turle. 'The others were in by half-
past six: I saw them walking on the grass, which you
must not.'

'All the trains were late.'

'Hmn,' said Turle, through his nose, in the proper
and famous Turtle way: the next remark after Hmn
was always a verse from the day's psalms. ' "In the
evening they will return: grin like a dog and will go
about the city",' said Turle. 'Come on, Owen, I'm
not holding this door open all night.'

Owen stepped through the postern: it was a small
door in a larger one, so there was a sill a foot high to
lift your feet over. Turle closed the postern and locked
it, turned away in silence and went turtle-walking
into his own house beside the gate.

Owen was left standing in the dark archway alone. There was only a cat watching a ray of light filtering through the keyhole of the big gate. 'Puss,' he said, 'Tinker, Tinker,' because that was the name of the cat at home. But this cat had no name like it: it ran out into the Precincts, over a wall and away.

Coming through the postern, Owen had almost left behind him town and shops, home and holidays, other people and far places; these things were almost gone; but not entirely. The school term itself did not start for another week and a day. The Cathedral services had to be sung all the year round: so for half the holidays the day-boys sang, and for the other half of the holidays the boarders; and that meant staying after the end of term and returning before the beginning. At this moment the holidays were still on.

In front of Owen now there was the Cathedral, grey and soft in starry light. It stood in grass like a ship anchored in a green swell: the uneven lawns swept away from the walls in bow waves and eddies, flurries and wakes; yet nothing moved, and across the tides of grass was stretched in two or three places a gangplank of a path to a door. Above the door there would be a window eighty times its size; so that the people going in and out of the door looked like ants at the entrance to their own tiny terraces. Now the building was dark and empty. The windows were as solid as the walls, and the most solid parts of the whole were the shadows between the buttresses and behind the outrigged chapels. High above the shadowed hull rose the tower, like a mast full of sail; and the lights from the town came over the houses and lit up the traced arches, the channelled corners, and the four golden wind-flags on the turrets above the corners.

Owen walked round the Cathedral on the gravel, passing the round east end walking on the grass, because his feet made too insolent a noise on the path: in all the rest of the Precincts there was silence, until the Cathedral clock rang the ten notes of the three quarters; and the sound sang above the roof and round the tall tower and the four smaller ones for a hundred seconds afterwards.

Before the notes were swallowed into the sky, Owen came to the school, in a corner almost against the Cathedral. There was a wall that stretched round and across to the Cathedral, so that the building could, if you liked, be considered part of the Cathedral. Owen went in through the back door, the usual way, and found the lights on in the passage. He hung up his cap and coat, and changed into his house-shoes: still there was silence in the house.

He set out to find Mr Ardent, the headmaster, who was sure to be in the house somewhere; but before he came to the spiral staircase he heard two people coming down. He waited. Mr Ardent came first, saying over his shoulder, 'I think, Tom, that Trembling Timmy should *not* all the time be behind the same two boys. He makes them wobble as much as he does himself.'

Owen knew he was talking to Dr Sunderland, the organist, about the Lay Clerks: that is, the men of the Cathedral Choir, not the boys.

Dr Sunderland was fat, like Turle; they lived next door to each other, so they were sometimes called Tweedledum and Tweedledee. But Dr Sunderland was not in the least turtlish: he was more like a puffed gorilla. He was out of breath now, from coming down the spiral staircase too quickly.

'Man oughtn't 'mph choir at all,' he said, running out of breath on words that didn't matter. 'Positimph nuisance. Sings all over the 'mph, like 'mph little girl; squeaked 'mphmatins yestermph, like tom-cat 'mph prowl.'

He was talking to nobody because Mr Ardent had seen Owen waiting for him.

'Good evening, sir,' said Owen.

'Hello, Owen,' said Mr Ardent. 'A lost sheep. You came on the nine-twenty-eight, I suppose. Have you had any supper?'

'I did have some once,' said Owen, feeling very hungry indeed.

'You mean you wouldn't mind another innings? Dr Sunderland and I haven't finished our first yet, so come on.'

'Decidedlimph,' said Dr Sunderland. ''Mph, Owen.'

'Good evening, sir,' said Owen: that was what Dr Sunderland meant.

'Owen, take my cassock to the hall, and bring back my jacket, will you?' said Mr Ardent. 'We shall be in the kitchen.' He took off his cassock, and Owen slung it over his arm. Dr Sunderland lifted a large and gorilla-like hand and tugged the hindmost tuft of hair on Owen's head, and said ''Mph' which meant he was glad to see you: he was always glad to see everybody.

When Owen came back into the kitchen, there was the large frying-pan on the gas, Mr Ardent was beating six eggs in a basin with a fork, and Dr Sunderland was carrying the broken shells to the sink-tray, half a shell at a time, thoughtfully. Thoughtful about something else: twice he brought half a shell back, so he made fourteen journeys altogether.

'Tom, the toast,' said Mr Ardent.

''Mph?' said Dr Sunderland.' ''Mph toast, Owen.'

Owen rescued it from the grill and turned it over. Mr Ardent put a little milk in with the eggs, and then a little more pepper. Owen put the toast to keep warm, and started two more slices. Dr Sunderland stood up straight by the sink: his hands hung practically at his knees.

'Strict order 'mph seniority,' he said. 'Owen.'

'Yes, sir,' Owen, not understanding at once.

'Strict order 'mph seniority. What is it? Tell me. Start 'mph youngest.'

'There isn't anybody after the youngest,' said Owen.

'Idiomph,' said Dr Sunderland. 'Ascending order.'

'Champlin, Arnold, Arle, Underwood, Linkley . . .' Owen began.

'Start youngest 'mph Singing Boy 'mph boarders

here, not with the youngest in 'mph school,' said Dr Sunderland.

'Crew, Owen, Iddingley, Dubnet . . .'

'Enough,' said Dr Sunderland. 'Crew's the sting in the tail, is he?'

'He's Beekeeper, yes, sir,' said Owen.

The youngest Singing Boy of the Cathedral was always called the Beekeeper, though for four hundred years there had been no bees to be kept.

'Weird story, that,' said Dr Sunderland.

'A very odd thing to do,' said Mr Ardent. 'A perfectly idle custom, and a great nuisance to everybody: and all for the sake of saying you don't know where something is, but you've got something that will do just as well. Is that pan hot enough, do you think?'

He tipped the basin of beaten egg into the smoking frying-pan. The yellow mixture went in with a great sizzle, swirling round on the hot fat in great peninsular continents, until it met itself, and joined up into a disc and began to blow blisters.

'It looks like the prehistoric moon, sir,' said Owen. 'That was all round and all volcanoes.'

'Just as round, but not so edible as Choir School omelette,' said Mr Ardent. He pulled in the hem of the omelette and let the liquid centre flow to the edges. Then he folded the whole thing in two, sliced it in three, and scooped one piece on to each plate.

'Toast-master Owen, dish out the toast,' said Mr Ardent. He turned out the hissing gas, and there was quiet except for a chair whimpering under Dr Sunderland, and the big bell called St Dunstan tumbling out ten o'clock.

'Ever tried 'mph honey omelette?' said Dr Sunderland. 'We'll try 'mph in the autumn, Edward, with a new honeycomb.'

'Don't ask me to help you take it from the hive,' said Mr Ardent. 'They set themselves against me round about. My hide isn't an inch thick.'

'Got to eat 'mph at once,' said Dr Sunderland. 'Whilst 'mph still warm. Advantages 'mph having serious mind 'mph not being paid enough wages. Organist and wax supplier to 'mph Cathedral.'

Dr Sunderland kept bees because it amused him and he liked honey, not because he had to supply wax for the Cathedral candles. Many years ago the organist of the Cathedral had to make the candles himself and supply his own wax. Nowadays the candles were bought from a warehouse, and were no longer made of beeswax; nor were so many needed, because the Cathedral was lit by electricity, and only altars and processions needed candles.

Before the days when the organist had had to make the candles, one of the priors of the monastery, Prior Tollelege, had kept large numbers of bees, no one knew where. Each year, on the Sunday after Ascension Day, the youngest Singing Boy had taken a candle made from the Prior's beeswax to the bishop for inspection, so that the bishop could be certain that there were enough candles to carry out the services properly.

The youngest Singing Boy had done it, because he was the smallest, and he could get up among the hives through an entrance too small for the monks. The boy gathered the wax and the honey, and once a year brought out a swarm of bees, to show the bishop, along with the candle.

When the Prior had left and the monastery been emptied in the time of Henry VIII, the bees had been forgotten; but the youngest Singing Boy was still called the Beekeeper, and at matins on the Sunday after Ascension Day, he still brought a candle to the bishop at his throne, and assured him that the organist was still carrying out his duties and supplying wax, although the bees were lost.

'Crew, Owen, Iddingley, Dubnet . . .' said Dr Sunderland. 'It'll have to 'mph Owen.'

'John Owen, Beekeeper,' said Mr Ardent. 'Iddingley is a small man, though not so young.'

'Much smaller,' said Dr Sunderland. 'Loud voice.' He chased the last piece of his omelette round the plate with his toast, and cornered it against the fork; it was a large piece of omelette, and it hung over the prongs of the fork like a quilt on a hedge. Dr Sunderland opened his mouth with a grunt, and swallowed omelette and toast and seemed in danger of swallowing the fork as well.

'Owen's privilege,' said Mr Ardent. 'But we'll discuss it, and the rates of pay, in the morning.'

'Five 'mph a year,' said Dr Sunderland. Owen knew that 'mph meant pounds; five pounds a year was a good thing.

'But what about Crew?' he asked.

'Stung by a mumps germ,' said Mr Ardent. 'I'm glad he didn't bring the affliction back with him. If you've finished, Owen, you'd better run along to bed. Do wash off that third eyebrow adorning your left cheek.'

'Train dirt,' said Owen, finding most of the eyebrow on his fingers when he touched it. Dr Sunderland touched his own chin experimentally, but the swarthiness that surrounded his face was due to hard-growing black beard that always showed no matter how often he shaved.

''Mph,' said Dr Sunderland, meaning, 'Good night, and don't start growing a beard.'

Owen took his case and went up the spiral staircase to the dormitory. He found all the best beds already taken: he expected that, because you could choose your bed and sleep where you liked until term began and the juniors came back, and he was the last comer with no choice.

'Who's that?' said the largest bed. 'Mumpy Crew?'

'Me: Owen. Which bed can I have, please, Trevithic?'

'Sleep on the floor,' said Trevithic. 'Or right over in the corner. Why are you late?'

'Trains were late,' said Owen.

'Welsh trains always are,' said Trevithic.

'They don't want to hurry into a stupid dump like England,' said Owen. He felt safe, with Trevithic at the other end of the dormitory in bed. Trevithic was a Cornishman, and he agreed that England was a stupid dump; but pointed out that Wales was worse. 'It's a dull passage,' he said, using Dr Sunderland's description of anything he might not like in a piece of music.

'I've just had supper with Mr Ardent and Tweedledum,' said Owen.

Dubnet woke up then, and managed to say: 'Did he tell you you'd got to be Beekeeper?' before going straight to sleep again on his face.

'He'll tell me in the morning,' said Owen. 'But I don't see why it matters particularly: you don't have to *do* anything.'

'You'll get paid next Sunday,' said Trevithic. 'In the Treasury, after matins.'

'Five pounds,' said Owen. 'Well done, ye!' That was a Choir School phrase: no one knew who had invented it. It was a sign of joy and approval.

'You've only got to talk to the Bishop and sing an introit,' said Trevithic. 'It's really good pay and no chiz; better than one pound fifty for a wedding.'

'Crew will be back by then,' said Owen, but he knew as he said it that he was wrong. Even in the dark dormitory, now, he saw Trevithic's face looking towards him with scorn.

'*You* are a dull passage,' said Trevithic. 'Crew won't be back by next Sunday. Didn't Tweedledum tell you? What do you think they're arranging it now for?'

'Oh well, I forgot,' said Owen, getting into bed in the dark, and making a determination that he would not be Beekeeper. Even if the Bishop and Dr Sunderland, and Trevithic as Head Chorister, came to the choir stalls and pulled him out in cassock and surplice, he would bite his ruff and not sing. And he went on biting, so that when he woke up the corner of the collar of his pyjamas was still in his mouth, cold and wet; but he had pulled it out before the bell that woke him had stopped ringing.

'Look, here's Owen,' said Iddingley, while everybody else was looking under the beds for their slippers.

'He got here at midnight,' said Dubnet. 'Waking everybody up.' Nobody ever listened to all that Dubnet had to say, so nobody contradicted him.

'They had to push the train all the way from Wales,' said Trevithic. 'Taffy-was-a-Welshman had stolen the wheels.'

'Well done, ye,' said Kelsey, looking round for someone to pick a quarrel with, but there was only Dubnet left and the others had gone to wash; and no one could quarrel with Dubnet who was too easily persuaded he was wrong. Dubnet went to wash, Kelsey changed Trevithic's clothes with Madington's, and went after the others.

Trevithic and Madington decided that Silverman had changed the clothes about, so, dressed in each other's shirts they tied Silverman up in his own sheets with his own dressing-gown cord. The result was that Kelsey had to lay the breakfast tables out of turn instead of Silverman, who was still upstairs untying himself and making his bed.

At breakfast Mr Ardent made the arrangements for the day: choir practice at 8.40, service at 9.30, and after service everyone to practise musical instruments, whichever they played, but that was only a quarter of an hour each; and after that nobody had any duties at all until ten to one, and if it was your turn you helped serve dinner, and if it wasn't you came in at one o'clock and ate it.

It was a long breakfast today, because Mr Ardent had to make up the piano and violin practice list, with choice of best times in order of seniority. Owen found himself left with the worst time of all, right in the middle of the morning's free time, at twelve o'clock.

'Or you can do it before breakfast if you feel resolute enough,' said Mr Ardent. 'And you'll have the bees to keep, Owen.'

'Buzz, buzz, buzz, I wonder why he does, sir,' said Trevithic.

'Buzzent, buzzent, buzzent, I wonder why he doesn't,' said Dubnet, who saw Owen about to refuse; but nobody heard Dubnet, and Mr Ardent said: 'We'll discuss it after service, Owen. And after service will all those whose trunks have come go to the linen-room and see when they can be unpacked.'

Then everybody stood for grace. Madington reminded Mr Ardent that there was plenty of time for extra French and Latin.

'Extra French and Latin,' said Mr Ardent, beginning

another announcement in the doorway. 'We must try and crowd some into this week. What did you say, Iddingley?'

'Down with Madington, sir,' said Iddingley. Mr Ardent laughed, and Iddingley went to stand nearest to the other door, to be as far as possible as soon as possible from Madington.

'I've kept you long enough already,' said Mr Ardent. 'We'll discuss Latin and French at dinner-time. Iddingley, don't let me forget.'

'Ooh, yes, sir,' said Iddingley.

Just before twenty to nine the bell rang: a signal to assemble in the yard in a single file ready to walk across into the Cathedral.

There was blue sky round the roof; the sun was behind the great centre tower of the Cathedral. A puff of cloud lay over the pinnacle of one of the smaller towers – one of the pair of little square towers that grew behind the crosswings of the Cathedral and went up plain and square and unbuttressed, and only grew into lone-standing towers for a few feet at their tops. They went up into pointed lead roofs that peeped at each other over the long spine of the Cathedral; but they had nothing to say across the steep ridge between them: they might have forgotten each other since the building had risen there.

Trevithic gave the order to march: 'Left, left, left,' and the cloud sank behind the Cathedral. The file turned right; Trevithic walked beside it giving the step; Owen came last, going not left, right, left, right, but two rights and then two lefts and hopping from side to side, imagining himself the tail of a dragon.

The dragon went up the steps on thirty-two feet, through a door, and found itself in the Cathedral. Owen stopped being the tail of a dragon, and became the youngest but not the smallest choirboy: Iddingley, just in front, was the smallest. Owen wondered whether Iddingley would like to become Beekeeper: he had a loud voice and he would not mind at all being the only talker in the Cathedral, or even the only singer. Owen had more dread than anyone else of being asked to sing a solo: even the short Introit sung by the Beekeeper to the Bishop.

The file stopped at the bottom of the steps that led up inside a wall to the hidden practice room. Trevithic came to the head of the file and led the way up. The file went up slowly. While Owen waited at the end, Dr Sunderland came heavily and darkly up, and waited to be last, so that he could go at his own speed.

''Mph morning,' he said, and leaned against the wall. 'How's the Beekeeper?'

'All right, thank you, sir,' said Owen, offering him his place.

''Mph follow you,' said Dr Sunderland. He always walked up the narrow stair sideways with no one watching. 'D'you know 'mph Introit 'mph sing Bishop?'

'We heard it last year when Kelsey did it, sir,' said Owen.

'Beastly thing,' said Dr Sunderland.

'Yes, sir,' said Owen. He said it fervently, hoping

that Iddingley would be inspired to volunteer to sing it instead. Iddingley turned round and said, 'It's filthy, sir. Not interesting.'

'Pleasant tune,' said Dr Sunderland. 'Only fault 'mph's unaccompanied.' Above all, Dr Sunderland enjoyed making a noise on the organ. 'Not a dull passage, but undeveloped, Iddinglmph.'

'Yes, sir,' said Iddingley.

Owen knew the chance had gone: Iddingley would not volunteer to be Beekeeper. So the task was one of those things that could not be avoided, except by mumps. Mr Ardent knew that, and he knew exactly what you thought about singing solos, and your opinion of other essential and unattractive tasks. If you tried to argue, he gave you at once undeniable reasons why you were the very person for the job, and made you feel that if you didn't do it you would come to a thing called a sticky end: obviously drowning in treacle, or being tarred and feathered.

'Go 'mph,' said Dr Sunderland. Owen went up and stood at his place. Dr Sunderland followed slowly, stood in the doorway for a moment like an amiable gorilla, and said in a very pleasant, cordial and sunny-morning way, ''Mph.'

Hear My Voice

DENNIS HAMLEY

'Oh, go on, sir. Let's not have the summer concert in the boring old school hall. Let's take it outside.'

Mr Wycherley sighed. He was Head of Music and his senior choir was being very stroppy.

'Yeah. Let's get out of this rotten old dump.'

'Outside in the sunshine. That's where we ought to be. Like the Kings' Singers in punts floating down the river.'

Mr Wycherley had a good-natured revolt on his hands. Privately, he agreed with it. Like most secondary school halls, theirs was hardly the Barbican Centre. Perhaps, while he played for time, sarcasm might be his best weapon.

'Where do you suggest?' he inquired. 'Shall we turn the tennis-courts into the Hollywood Bowl? String quartets in the long-jump pit? I'm always open to sensible suggestions.' He ignored the ripple of derisive laughter which greeted the last remark.

'Leo's Tump;' said a quiet voice beside him.

'I beg your pardon,' said Mr Wycherley.

He looked down to his right, where Colin Chiltern sat at the piano.

'Leo's Tump, sir,' said Colin. 'It's on Wilcox's farm.'

'What on earth is Leo's Tump?' said Mr Wycherley.

There was an immediate buzz of approval from the choir.

'Great idea, Colin.'

'That would be *really* good.'

'Let's get out there now.'

Mr Wycherley tapped with his baton on his music stand for quiet.

'Now,' he said, 'before we have a mass exodus, will somebody please tell me what Leo's Tump is? Or who Leo Stump is, for that matter.'

'It's a little hill, sir,' said Colin.

'It's not even that,' said a girl in the choir. 'It's just a tiny bump. Like a little cape at a bend in the river.'

'It's not even a river,' said a boy in the basses. 'It's only a brook.'

'Leo's Tump seems to be getting progressively smaller,' said Mr Wycherley. 'What is this mysterious quality which makes it so suitable for musical performance?'

Colin spoke.

'It's on this bend in the river,' he said. 'It's like a grassy bank shaded by willow trees. It's not that small.

You could have the whole choir sitting on the grass at the top and the orchestra on the flat bit at the bottom easily. And the audience could sit in the meadow on the other side of the river.'

'Marvellous,' said Mr Wycherley. 'And how are we to get a piano out there? They are quite heavy, you know.'

'Actually,' said Colin, 'we could borrow an electronic piano. The fifth-year rock group have got one. It wouldn't be nearly as heavy. Anyway, they'll be playing too. They wouldn't mind lending it.'

Now Mr Wycherley was really sarcastic.

'I see,' he said. 'I didn't realize Leo's Tump was so eminently suitable. How thoughtful of Nature to provide the willow trees with a 240 volt electricity supply and a sufficiency of 13 amp sockets.'

There was more laughter – dutiful this time. 'Sir's made a funny,' an unidentifiable voice said.

Colin continued patiently and quite seriously. 'No trouble. The electricity's dead easy.'

Blast Chiltern. Why did he have to be so practical as well as so incredibly talented?

'Go on,' said Mr Wycherley. 'Amaze me yet again.'

'Leo's Tump is on Mr Wilcox's land. It's only a hundred yards away from his cowsheds and milking stalls. We could easily get some heavy-duty extension leads.'

'Oh, yes? And what about Mr Wilcox? Does he have a say in all this?'

'He's Karen Wilcox's father,' said Colin. 'She's in the third year. He's Chairman of the PTA. And he's putting up for the District Council next elections. He'd be dead chuffed about it. It'd get his name known among the voters.'

'Ah, well,' said Mr Wycherley. '"There is a tide in the affairs of men" as the English Department would say. I'll think about it. And I'll have a word with the Head.'

The choir cheered.

'You won't regret it, sir,' said Colin.

'All right, then. Settle down.' Mr Wycherley was the efficient conductor once again. 'From the start. *Non Nobis Domine*.'

The choir groaned.

'I'll write something specially for the concert,' said Colin. 'World *première* at Leo's Tump.'

Yes, thought Mr Wycherley. Colin Chiltern will write something for the concert. And it will be superb. Mr Wycherley felt the pride of the good teacher in a brilliant pupil. And Colin Chiltern was a prodigy. A brilliant pianist, violinist, flautist – and a composer whose mastery of form, harmony, melody, were way beyond his years. Could Mozart have been any more competent at the same age? Mr Wycherley could not see how. Colin Chiltern ought (or so some thought) to be at a specialist music school or the Royal College. But his parents would have none of it. They kept him on at the local comprehensive where he remained happy and well liked in spite of – or perhaps because of – his huge and extraordinary talent.

Brother Leofric's stone cell was cold at the best of times; the quiet morning hours after matins on a snowy, lowering January day meant a particular bone-rotting bitterness for the old monk. Arthritis over the years had crippled his fingers so that it was a wonder he could still hold his brush as he worked painstakingly at the illuminations on the parchment. But what he had lost in dexterity he had kept in cunning and the blinding ropes of colour crept surely across the page as they had always done.

De Profundis. The one hundred and thirtieth psalm. *Out of the deep have I called unto you, O Lord. Lord hear my voice.*

His cracked old voice chanted the words in his beloved Latin. *Lord, hear my voice.*

Brother Leofric was scribe for the monastery. *De Profundis* he was copying: a copy to be the King of all copies and to be presented to the archbishop himself one day. So the script was the most painstaking and the illuminations were the most intricate, the most colourful, the most beautiful that even he, Brother Leofric of the sure though shaking hand, had ever been responsible for. Which meant it would be unmatched anywhere.

Out of the deep. The words sounded in the cell. *Lord,*

hear my voice. The old man in the coarse brown habit sang softly to himself.

De profundis. The reds and greens and golds and purples twined snake-like over the page. The great letter D and the lesser E to start the page took shape. In the middle of the greater letter D under Brother Leofric's cunning hand there began to form a mouth: between its lips, a tongue. *Hear my voice*. Brother Leofric sang again, repetitively. The mouth grew on the parchment.

Colin Chiltern sat at the piano in the living-room of his home. A neat pile of manuscript paper rested on top of the piano: loose sheets covered with music were placed carefully on the floor by the stool. He wrote on the sheet before him as he tried melodies, phrases and harmonies. He was very happy.

He had decided what he would write. A four-part unaccompanied anthem for the school choir. In whose style should it be? He surveyed the list of English composers he most admired: Gibbons, Tallis, Byrd, Purcell, Elgar, Britten. All of them and none. Their harmonies filled his mind. But as soon as he put pen to paper he was his own man. The style was of them all, yet it was his own. He had soon decided what words he would use. They were words which – from his earliest years singing in the church choir – had fascinated him. Psalm 130. The first verse and a half only.

Out of the deep have I called unto thee, O Lord.
Lord, hear my voice.
Out of the deep:

What marvellous rising, straining, urgent musical phrases those words conjured up. The deep of what? The deep, dark silent places of the sea? The hidden deeps of the mind? Yes. A rising, repeated figure starting quiet and deep with the basses as if from a formless void: taken up by the tenors and getting louder, faster and clearer but with the basses forming an underlying, satisfying harmony: then on to the altos, faster still and more ornate, with the underlying harmonies now thicker, fuller: finally a climax with the sopranos, spreading over four octaves and culminating in a rich, full statement. His fingers trembled with joy as the notes spread across the manuscript paper; his mind exulted as he reproduced an interior performance which could fill the Albert Hall or make the echoes ring for miles and miles around Leo's Tump. And that other phrase. *Hear my voice.* What a superb three words they were. He turned them in his mind into a multitude of quick three-note phrases, tossed from bass to tenor, tenor to soprano, soprano back down to alto like a flowing passing movement in a football match.

Yes, his anthem would be wonderful. A beautiful object made from nothing. No one else could do it.

It's quite extraordinary, thought Mr Wycherley.

Those kids couldn't be more right. Leo's Tump was even better than they had described. The sweep of the river, the promontory which was the Tump itself, the sloping, concave lie of the meadow opposite, all combined to turn the place into a natural amphi-theatre. Now he had seen it, he was full of the idea.

Mr Wilcox had been very co-operative. He had offered car-parking in the next field, full use of the electricity supply in his cowsheds as well as his own heavy-duty extension leads and all the rehearsal time on the Tump the school needed.

'All you want now is the weather,' he said.

'The place is so perfect that if we don't get the right weather on the night, we'll wait till we do,' said Mr Wycherley.

The two men stood on the top of the Tump looking down the river.

'Why is it called Leo's Tump?' asked Mr Wych-erley.

'No one rightly knows,' said Mr Wilcox. 'I think it's something to do with the old monastery.'

'I didn't know there was one,' said Mr Wycherley.

'It's gone, years ago. You can still see the earthworks and a few old stones two miles downstream.'

'But why Leo?'

'I did hear once an old story about some monk called Leo who managed to raise the devil.'

'So?'

'They're both under the Tump.'

'I hope they never get out,' said Mr Wycherley.

93

The two men walked together away from the Tump and down to the pub.

Leofric's cell was very small: the stone walls were feet thick. The grey misty light which filtered in through the high glassless window gave little light: sometimes being in the cell was like sitting in a tiny box at the centre of the earth.

So when Leofric heard an echo to his cracked old voice as it sang its little plainsong refrain over and over again while his hands worked busily he said to himself, 'Strange. I have heard echoes in the chapel and the refectory and even outside among the hills. But never in my cell.'

And all the while, the mouth with its lips and its tongue took shape. And the echo grew more distinct. *Hear my voice.*

It was not an echo. It was a separate voice.

The mouth was complete. Its lips were curved, hooked, cruel. Its tongue was barbed, like a serpent told of in some traveller's tale.

Hear my voice. Hear my voice. The voice was shrill, demented, biting deep into Brother Leofric's mind. He dropped his brush, placed his hands over his ears and stared at the complete mouth that had appeared on the page through his cunning hand but which he had never, never intended.

Hear my voice.

The little cell was full of deafening sound. He

clapped his hands even tighter to his ears. To no avail.

He screamed to drown the noise but could not even hear himself. He bent downward to pick the parchment up. It seemed to crackle back at him with a force of its own. Shooting pains entered his fingers and ran along his arms. He staggered out of his cell holding the parchment in front of him like a shield. His sandals flapped over the stones and his fellow monks emerged from their cells or stopped their work outside to stare strangely at him.

'What have I done?' he cried. 'Have I been too proud?'

The voice beat on in his ears. *Hear my voice. Hear my voice.* But no other monk came over to Leofric: no other monk gave any sign of having heard it. Brother Leofric stumbled on, out of the monastery, over the snow-covered land to the dark river and then along its bank towards the hills far away.

I will lift up my eyes to the hills. His mind wanted him to chant the words to combat the hideous, hideous *hear my voice.* But his vocal cords could not move: he made no sounds beyond retching gasps for breath.

The weather at the end of June looked as though it was set fair for weeks. The first rehearsals at Leo's Tump showed even more clearly how good it was as an open-air theatre. Already there was talk of *A Midsummer Night's Dream* being put on there next year. Everything was rehearsed to perfection at the Tump –

except *Out of the Deep* by Colin Chiltern. The choir had practised it until they could sing it in their sleep. But Colin was adamant. The first performance was to be at Leo's Tump and it was to be the only one. His purist ear wanted to savour the particular sound of *Out of the Deep* in the open air to the accompaniment of the murmuring river just once and never again.

Back at school, though, the anthem had shaped well. The choir loved it and sang it with special affection because they knew it was written entirely for them and that it was music quite out of the ordinary.

The day approached. The weather stayed clear and hot. Chairs were brought up from the school and put in rows in the meadow. Music stands for the orchestra were set up on the little beach at the foot of the Tump. The extension leads were laid for the rock group (who weren't quite happy about the arrangement) and for the electronic piano.

Mr Wycherley watched it all happen under his direction and crossed his fingers. The logistics of setting up the concert each year were bad enough normally: he must have needed his head examined to make it all ten times worse. But if it went off well, wouldn't it be something to remember?

Well, he hoped so. But it would be Colin's night really. It was Colin's idea, and the centre-piece of the whole evening would be Colin's anthem. Mr Wycherley, in spite of himself, could not repress a pang of envy. By heck, that Colin Chiltern was a lucky one.

★

Hear my voice. The screaming, demented voice was changing. It grew quieter.

'Thank God,' breathed Brother Leofric.

It settled down to a whisper. But what a whisper. A whisper deep in the inner ear, so raw and rasping that it seemed to gouge out the ear-drum. And what a feeling accompanied it. For the words that were whispered in his ear and the mouth that whispered them seemed to belong to something that sat on the back of his neck, that squatted on his shoulders. Nothing was there: he *knew* nothing could be there. But this nothing was heavy; it weighed him down, it made him stop, stumble, lose his footing in the snow.

What had happened? Part of Brother Leofric's mind could still work clearly: it reasoned well and came up with the only answer. He had to tell everyone.

He turned.

Before him, watching him wonderingly but not leaving the precincts of the monastery, stood the monks. Leofric made a superhuman effort and his voice carried with desperate strength across the grey snow, almost as if the words he spoke were illumined on the parchment-grey breath which came from his mouth.

'Listen. Listen, my brothers. With my own art I have raised the fiend. Rather your hands should lose their cunning than you should raise him too.'

Leofric turned again and moved, now with awful slowness, through the snow towards the far hills.

★

The evening of the concert was here. The weather stayed perfect. Lines of cars drew up in the field Mr Wilcox had given for parking; the rows of seats in the meadow filled up with shirt-sleeved and summer-dressed parents and friends. The girls of the choir and orchestra arrived in their long dresses; the boys filed to their places in their dark grey trousers and white shirts. To Mr Wycherley, moving to the conductor's stand for Schubert's *Marche Militaire*, the whole scene looked comfortingly familiar yet – framed by the willow trees, the far hills and the blue sky, the audience separated from the performers by a running river – uneasily different.

Leofric could go no further. The weight of whatever thing it was gripping the back of his neck and whispering in his ear was too much to bear. He sank to his knees and wept.

Then, above the whispering, he heard a voice shouting from far off.

'Leofric. Leofric.'

With his last strength, he turned. A burly figure, also in a brown habit, was running towards him, leaving untidy footprints in the wet snow. With a leap of the heart, Leofric recognized him. It was his Abbot. In him, thought Leofric, I put my trust.

'What is happening, old friend?'

Leofric looked up at the Abbot with piteous eyes.

'The fiend,' he whispered.

Could the Abbot see what Leofric felt on the back

of his neck? Leofric did not know. But the Abbot's eyes showed understanding.

'Come on, old friend. Back to the monastery.'

'No,' gasped Leofric. 'I must carry this scourge far away.'

'Then I will come with you.'

The Abbot looped his huge arm round Leofric's thin shoulders and pulled him on his way. He saw the parchment manuscript with the mouth on it but said nothing. They trudged on.

He stopped suddenly, and Leofric stopped with him. They stood on a little hill which overlooked a bend in the river. All around them was deserted whiteness.

'Stop here, Leofric,' said the Abbot. 'Lay down your burden.'

Out of the deep was the last item of the concert. When he had come to arrange the programme, Mr Wycherley could think of no more fitting finale. Colin stood alone at the conductor's stand, facing his singers. He played the commencing note; then raised his arms to bring the basses in and start the deep rhythmic murmur which set the anthem in motion.

'I cannot,' said Leofric. 'I cannot lay it down. The burden is with me for ever.'

He felt the grip of the thing on the back of his neck tighten even further: the whispering kept on and on.

'Then I will help you, Leofric,' said the Abbot.

He faced Leofric, looking him square in the eyes. He made the sign of the cross and then cried out in Latin the great prayer of exorcism.

The whispering in Leofric's ear stopped. It changed again – to a scream, without words, which rose shrilly. The grip tightened – but its feel was changed, as if now the thing was clinging on desperately.

The anthem reached its half-way point. The opening words – *Out of the deep have I called unto thee, Oh Lord* – had ended in that full, rich affirmative chord Colin's fingers had trembled to write. The sound of his own music was such that the back hairs on his scalp rose and tears of joy welled at the back of his eyes.

Now the chasing three-note figure of the words *Hear my voice* were to start the final part. His ears almost ached with the anticipation of hearing his work again.

Leofric listened. Quiet at first but growing louder came a strange, full, unearthly music such as he had never heard. In the background he could hear the Abbot still chanting the prayer of exorcism, casting out the unclean spirit. But the new music soon flooded his being and he stared down in wonder to the river from where it seemed to come. There a figure mistily stood: a figure in black and white, around whom the music seemed to radiate.

The intricate, extraordinary sounds floated round Brother Leofric's mind like a patterned design. The different melodies took on colours to him. The girls' high voices were a bright gold: the girls' lower notes were a warm red. The high men's notes were a fierce sky blue: the bass voices a rich purple. The coloured ropes of sound twined round his brain until Colin Chiltern's anthem heard from over the centuries turned into one of his own illuminations.

The thing on the back of his neck loosened its grip. And now Leofric heard words in the music – *Hear my voice* – and he knew what would happen. The thing detached itself from his neck. For the first time he saw it, squat, slime-green, foul. And it hopped obscenely towards its new prize, the misty figure in black and white, while its renewed whispers of *Hear my voice* seemed to merge with that sweet music.

They had reached the final cadences. As the music swept all round him, Colin closed his eyes, making the notes a disembodied, pure sound. But with his eyes closed he saw a different sight in front of him. The Tump was still there – but on it were two brown-habited men. One clasped his hands together and seemed to be shouting at the sky. The other, nearer, was old. He stared straight at Colin, a beseeching fear in his eyes. And on the back of his neck sat a loathsome creature, slime-green and scaly, with black, dead eyes and a mouth with hooked and cruel lips and a barbed tongue.

Time seemed to stop. The anthem froze in his mind. No longer was it something which moved from beginning to end in the space of four minutes. He saw it all at once, like an intricate design, the melodies like twining, coloured lines, making a delicately shaped framework with a space in the middle.

Through the space he could see the old man with the creature on his back. And when the framework was complete, the creature left the old man and hopped towards him. The dead eyes looked at him, the barbed tongue flicked, the mouth whispered, *Hear my voice.*

The sound bit into Colin's ears. He felt claws dig hard into his shoulders and neck as the creature took up its place. Colin staggered under the weight: he seemed to lose balance. It was as if a sudden roaring sheet of flame engulfed him and he was hurled into a deep abyss.

The Abbot thought they had been struck by lightning. He reeled under the simultaneous blinding flash and reverberating clap and then stared incredulously at the great crack in the ground which appeared at his feet. He looked at Leofric, who lay on the ground, a look almost of peace in his eyes.

'It has left me,' the old man said.

The parchment he had carried all this time lay beside him. A sudden gust of wind lifted it: down into the fissure it fluttered and lay there, four feet deep with the painted mouth facing upward.

'Where has the fiend gone to?' asked Leofric.

'I do not know,' said the Abbot.

'I brought him forth.' Leofric tried to rise, then sank back. 'I thought my gifts raised me above other men. So he came to me.'

He lay still, his eyes open and staring. The Abbot watched for a moment, then bent down and gently closed the lids.

'Now, old friend,' he said, 'this is your resting place. You must be left with the companion you brought into the world. I cannot take you back with me to our holy ground.'

He cradled the old, dead man in his arms and laid him in the crack in the ground.

'Goodbye, Leofric,' he said. 'We will come back to give you proper burial.'

Nobody was ever sure what happened as the anthem reached its end. Some said there must have been a shaft of summer lightning which sprang without warning from the sky and struck Colin down as the last chord of his great anthem sounded through the air. Others said the strain of seeing the concert right through to the end was too much for him and he had a mild stroke. At any rate, without warning, he staggered, fell and lay unconscious while the choir rushed round him and Mr Wilcox ran as hard as he could to the house to ring for an ambulance. In their horror, all the members of the audience forgot the beauty of the anthem, though afterwards they would recall it with burning clarity.

A month passed. Colin had been very ill. Now he was up and about again, but he seemed to have a stoop which indicated that he might indeed have suffered a slight stroke. Today, for the first time since before the concert, he sat at his piano. He placed some manuscript paper on the table by his side. He was going to compose again.

He opened his mind to let the music in and his hands rested on the piano keys. He was aware of a weight on the back of his neck, as of something he could not see but knew always to be there, ready at his ear to whisper.

And slowly the music came. It came in discords and it came in deep gruff snatches which could not be called melodies. It came in howls and shrieks as from some dark and secret place of terror. It came without beauty and without joy, as if telling truths which he could not understand but which he had to express. It filtered its way out of his mind through his fingers on to the keys and then into notes on the manuscript paper so that the truths were frozen for ever. And it came compulsively and with an unreasoning power, to be written down at once, though every note that jerked itself from him was hard and bitter agony.

★

The weather changed. A windy, cold summer gave way to an early, dark autumn. Mr Wycherley grieved for his pupil.

He missed the joy of seeing the long, clean-nailed fingers scamper across the piano keys; of finding on the neatly scribed manuscript paper marvellous music no one had heard before; of talk with one who knew instinctively what he himself had spent his whole life learning. Surely that superb mind had not been made to stop growing? Now there was just a tall boy with a stoop and dark eyes deep and morose. There was no talking, no laughter.

For month upon month, Mr Wycherley mused. What had struck Colin down? No answer came. Then, one night in February, he remembered. What had Mr Wilcox said that summer day? 'They're both under the Tump.' Yes, that was it. And one of them had got out. Was that crazy? No crazier than Colin coming to consciousness with all his music gone.

All that week he watched the silent, closed-up Colin Chiltern. He remembered the great ones of the past: Mozart and Schubert, dead in their prime; Beethoven so deaf he never heard his greatest work. And what about John Keats? Mr Wycherley thought of noble poets in their misery dead.

Yes, he knew what had happened to Colin Chiltern. And perhaps it had to.

Mr Wycherley never quite knew what made him,

that raw Sunday afternoon in February, put on his walking boots and cagoule and set out across the fields to Leo's Tump.

It was different now. The fields were muddy and squelched underfoot where melted snow and heavy rain had not drained away. The river itself flowed high and brown. The cows huddled together for warmth and the willow trees no longer bent over protectively but gestured in the stiff wind as if warning him off.

He stood below the Tump, on what was left above water of the little beach where he had conducted only last summer. He tried to see in his mind's eye the orchestra and choir and lifted his hands as if to set them off. But it was difficult to imagine music in this desolate place and all at once he felt foolish.

He was being watched. A dark figure in jeans, roll-neck jersey and donkey jacket was sitting under a willow tree, its back against the trunk, hands clasped round knees. It spoke.

'You won't hear the music and neither will I.'

Whatever is Colin doing at the Tump? thought Mr Wycherley. Does he come here regularly? Why?

'You will hear it, Colin,' he said. 'You will hear it again.'

Colin looked down on his teacher. You know nothing, he thought. You can't help me. No one can. Week after week I come here, to see if this thing will get off my back and go where it came from. If it doesn't go of its own accord I am past helping.

Mr Wycherley scrambled up the slope. Colin answered him without moving.

'I will never hear the music again,' he said.

Mr Wycherley squatted down beside him.

'You will, Colin, you will,' he said.

Colin turned dark eyes towards him but said nothing.

'Colin. I *know* what got out of the ground and entered your soul.'

No answer.

'Colin, tell me. Is the music just a noise? Just a rackety row?'

No answer again. But Colin's hands round his knees showed white as they gripped each other harder.

'And more than that. Do people you liked seem hateful? Is the world suddenly ugly? Cruel? Hopeless?'

No answer again. But the eyes widened.

'I'm right, aren't I, Colin? You don't need to say a word; I know I am. But this comes to everybody in the end, Colin. We all know sooner or later what the world is like. But it's come early to you. It's come before your time and without warning. It's hit you deep down inside and you can't sort it out.'

Colin spoke at last. His voice was thick and weary.

'Why me?'

Mr Wycherley's voice was urgent. Now he knew what to say.

'Colin, you're different from the rest of us. You

can see further and deeper than other people. One day your music will speak for them. You had harmony; now you've got noise. But the music can't die. The world has sorrow, yes, but the joy's still there. Keep listening to the noise, Colin. You'll make your art from the world as it is, not how you'd like it to be.'

Colin listened – both to Mr Wycherley and to his own mind. No, it was still noise. He closed his eyes.

He still seemed to see the Tump and the river below it. Two figures stood there. One was very tall and strongly built. The other stooped and was old. Both wore brown habits. They turned and looked at him.

Mr Wycherley still spoke and Colin still heard him.

'Keep listening to the noise. It will turn into music.'

The old man spoke as well.

'We have come back, Colin. That other time was not the end. I did not want to pass the fiend on to you. Better that he should have stayed with me. Forgive me, Colin.'

Then the Abbot spoke.

'A good man lies here,' he said. 'We gave him a proper burial. So where you sit is holy ground. The fiend will hurt you sorely. But he cannot conquer you. Hear *my* voice, Colin.'

Colin opened his eyes.

'Yes,' he said. 'I shall listen.'

He rose and walked away, without looking back. As he walked, he listened. Inside his mind the noise changed. The old harmonies did not return. But out of the cacophony there came, dimly at first but steadily stronger, a deeper, stranger music than he had ever heard before. He did not understand it; was not sure if he could handle it. But his pace quickened and soon he broke into a run, to lose no time in trying to capture it for ever.

The Glory Girl

BETSY BYARS

The Glory family bus rumbled along the highway. The old tyres wobbled. The engine missed. The windows and doors rattled. From time to time there was a loud bang as the engine backfired.

Anna Glory was stretched out on one of the back seats of the bus, trying to sleep. She lay on her side with her coat over her like a blanket. Down the aisle the pale-blue outfits of the Glory Gospel Singers waved and swayed on coat-hangers, giving off the faint odour of sweat and Right Guard.

The music her family had sung that night still sounded in Anna's head. The songs had been written that way – to start hands clapping, feet tapping, to make people want to join in on the chorus.

> *When He calls me,*
> *Calls me,*
> *Calls me,*

I will answer,
Answer,
Answer,
And I'll never,
Never,
Never,
Answer, 'No.'
Yes, when He calls me,
Calls me,
Calls me . . .

Anna closed her eyes. The music, the lights, the clapping, swaying crowd – it all seemed the way life was meant to be. And she at the back of the audi-torium, waiting to sell Glory albums and cassette tapes in the intermission – she felt left out, not just from the music and the crowd, but somehow from the rest of the world.

Anna sighed. She shifted on the hard seat. The Glory bus had once been a school bus, and the seats were worn slick from years of sliding, restless children.

Anna was the only person in the history of the Glory family who could not carry a tune. There had been a brief time, when Anna was seven, when it had been hoped that she could learn to play the drums.

Waiting for the drums to be delivered had been the happiest time of Anna's life. She had imagined how important she would look, beating time on the silver-and-blue Wilson drums, crossing her arms different ways, hitting this drum and that one.

But when the drums came and Anna held the sticks at last, she discovered that she could no more beat time than she could sing. She was clumsy. The drum-sticks clattered to the floor. Again and again her father shouted, 'Anna, listen to the music!'

And finally the drums had gone to the twins. They, at age five, took to it like monkeys, and before the week was out they were playing as if they had been doing it all their lives.

'Anyway, darling,' her father had said, 'we need you to sit at the back and sell records.'

'I don't want to sell records,' she'd said, starting to cry.

He'd looked at her. None of the children ever whined or pleaded when their father got that expression on his face. 'You'll get used to it,' he had said and then turned away.

It had been five years, however, and Anna had not got used to it yet.

She glanced up the aisle, past her mother's head which was lolling over the edge of the seat, past the twins' legs kicking at each other, past the gold of Angel's hair, to her father. Mr Glory was driving the bus, holding a Pall Mall cigarette between his teeth. He had to steer with his whole body.

Lately, the blue bus had started to take on a will of its own. It went left when it was supposed to go right, swerved into the dirt beside the road for no reason, and Mr Glory had to be ready for these unexpected moves. Mr Glory sometimes seemed to be dealing with a team of wilful mules instead of a bus.

He trusted the bus, though. 'It gets us there,' he would say when it was criticized for dying down at intersections or for stopping short and causing Mrs Glory to slide out of her seat. Mr Glory was proud that the bus had never had a flat, an oil change or a breakdown in all the years he had been driving it.

Anna's eyes closed. Pall Mall smoke drifted to the back of the bus and hung in the stale, cold air. On wet days Anna felt she could smell old peanut butter sandwiches and sneakers, and if she reached down under the seats she could feel knots of bubble gum so old they were as hard as the metal.

The Glory family's songs seemed to hang in the still, cold air of the bus, too.

> *Sing with the Glorys,*
> *Yes, come sing*
> *With the Glorys,*
> *If you sing*
> *With the Glorys*
> *Then you'll never*
> *Sing a-lone.*

When Anna heard that song, the Glory Gospel Singers' theme song, the last number on the programme, she would get up and move to the aisle where everybody could see her. Her father would step closer to the microphone, his guitar shifted out of the way, on his hip.

'Yes, ladies and gentlemen, if you've enjoyed

listening to the songs of the Glory Gospel Singers tonight, well, you can have all the songs you've heard on one long-playing album or cassette tape for the low, low price of eight dollars. That's a lot of singing for eight dollars.

'At the back of the auditorium one of the Glory girls, our little Anna – she can't sing, but ain't she pretty? – she'll be waiting to help you with your purchases. Hold up your hand, darling, so they can see where you're at.'

Dutifully Anna would hold up her hand, wave and then move back out of the light.

'And in the mean time, folks, remember, all the Glory family – Maudine, the twins Joshua and Matthew, our lead singer Angel and yours truly, John Glory – want you to –'

While Mr Glory was introducing the family, Anna would sit at her table and unlock her cash box. She would straighten the stacks of records and cassette tapes as inside the auditorium the music swelled.

> *Sing with the Glorys,*
> *Yes, come sing*
> *With the Glorys,*
> *If you sing*
> *With the Glorys*
> *Then you'll never,*
> *Never,*
> *Never!*
> *Siiiinnnnng a-lone!*

On the back seat of the bus, Anna pulled her coat up around her neck. She closed her eyes. Her body slid on the worn seat as the old bus stubbornly swerved to the left for no reason, and Mr Glory, with a puff on his Pall Mall, brought it back to the road again.

A Little Lower than
the Angels

GERALDINE MCCAUGHREAN

One moment he was holding them – the mallet in
one hand, the spike in the other – and the next
he was upside-down, hanging by one foot from the
rope. The loop closed round his ankle: he could feel
the hemp biting into his skin. His knee, thigh and
pelvis seemed on the point of parting company. He
was swinging, suspended, his arms flailing and his hair
hanging away from his skull. Blood hammered inside
his head.

The Mason, who had been standing underneath,
bent down and picked up the mallet and the spike and
weighed them in his hands. The sun shining through
the stained glass on to his pock-marked face turned it
a terrifying green and red. 'You mindless little toad.
You half-wit yard of kennel-water. You could have
done for me, dropping them!' He made as if to throw

the tools back up at the boy, but did not let go of them. There was nothing Gabriel could do to protect himself, strung up by one foot and just within the Mason's reach. He took hold of Gabriel's hair and set him swinging, so that the boy crashed against the wall. 'Look at you. What good are you, anyway? Look at your pretty yellow curls. If I'd wanted an apprentice with curls I'd have signed on a girl. Next time do me a favour – break your neck. Get him down, Squit.'

The second apprentice, Squit, squatting on the church floor with his head between his big, dirty knees, squinted up at Gabriel and thumbed his nose, babbling, 'Girl! Girl! Girl's got curls!'

Suddenly, hanging there from the roof of the church by one foot, waiting for that idiot Squit to slacken the rope and let him down, everything became horribly clear to Gabriel. It was like looking back on the route of a dreadful, uphill journey, from the last summit.

The Mason did not want an apprentice stonemason. He had never been interested in teaching his craft. Small boys irritated him. He could hardly stomach them near him. All the Mason wanted was the fee from Gabriel's parents, the twenty shillings they had paid to put the boy in the Mason's charge and have him taught a trade.

Now there was a second apprentice – Squit – and talk of a third. But the Mason did not teach. They learned anything they learned by watching him. They were given the arduous jobs – squaring off corners, rubbing down chisel marks, darkening down the Mason's accidental chips. And they saw precious little of the twenty shillings spent on food or clothing for either of them. It was true: if Gabriel had fallen and killed himself, he *would* have done the Mason a favour – made room for another apprentice, another twenty unearned shillings. Perhaps that was why he was hauled up to work with one foot in a loop of rope, instead of a basket like the Mason or fat Squit. Perhaps the Mason *wanted* him to have a fatal accident . . .

The thought made Gabriel want to shout out, 'Help! Don't let me die!' He wanted his parents. He wanted to break his apprentice's bond and go home. He hated himself for wanting it. Most of all, he hated himself for wanting to cry. He was glad that the blood turning him blue in the face and pounding in his eyeballs kept back the tears.

Squit loosed off the rope and let him fall hard to the floor head first. It was too much for Gabriel. He pressed the heels of his hands into his eye sockets, squatted back on his heels and sobbed. He was, after all, only eleven.

'If my father knew . . .' he began to say, meaning to share his flash of insight with Squit. But when he opened his eyes and took his hands away, Squit was far away, dancing round the nave singing, 'Girl! Girl! Girl's got curls!' And pushed close up against Gabriel's face was the Mason's pock-marked grin. 'Knew?

Knew what? That he's fathered a grizzling girl? 'Spect he's glad to be rid of you. I did him a favour. I got you away from that coddling mother of yours – always washing you – always slicking you like a cat. And we moved on, didn't we? We ben't going back, are we? You're bonded to me now, sure as a brand on a cow. You're mine, you smear of lard. Mine to spit on. Got it?' As his caked, yellow eyes travelled over Gabriel's face and head, what he saw caused him such disgust that his sweat-wet cheeks distorted as if they were melting. He searched for the worst insult in his huge mental library of insults and mouthed it into Gabriel's face through bared fangs. *'Pretty boy!'*

As Gabriel put his foot back into the rope loop and was hauled back up jerkily into the church roof, he felt too weary to hate the Mason. It took all the strength he could muster to despise himself – his pretty face, his curly hair, his cowardly tears. It was probably true: his father was probably glad to see the back of him. *Couldn't go home anyway. Don't know the way back*, he thought. He looked down at the church – at the green and red sunbeams falling on the Mason's scabby hair, and he thought, *How ridiculous. To think he would only take us for the bond money. Ridiculous. Too much blood in the brain, I suppose.*

The Mason brooded on the events of the day. Every time Gabriel looked round, he found the Mason's eyes on him. It made him nervous and clumsy.

Out of doors, excited people kept streaming past the church. Something out of the ordinary was happening. The Mason and his boys had to leave the church while a Mass took place. 'Feast day for some local saint,' he muttered, still eyeing Gabriel up and down contemptuously. Gabriel gathered that it was not so much the saint who was local as one of his bones, which rested in the church treasure chest and which once a year was taken out and venerated. The whole town took part – a holiday all of their own.

Squatting around in the muddy porch, wondering whether *he* was at the Mass or not, Gabriel watched the Mason eating bread and chives. He watched the Sacristan corner a stray dog in the side-chapel and throw it out of doors. He listened to the men gossiping near the door: on their knees or standing, they did not let the service interrupt their conversation.

'Well? Are you going?' said one.

'It's not Guild. It's not local men. Just a pack of gypsies. Not as good as locals,' said the other.

'Do it all year. Must be better. Stands to reason.'

'Do it all year? What kind of work's that? It's unholy, I call it.'

'Got the church steps, didn't they? Church must favour them.'

'Groat-and-farthing show,' said his friend suspiciously.

The first man left a moment's silence then said temptingly, 'You wouldn't believe Hell! I seen it on the road coming. Never seen a Hell like it!'

'Might stay, then. Might,' said his friend grudgingly.

'Did you hear that?' Gabriel whispered to Squit. '"Never seen a Hell like it." What's that mean?'

Squit had not been listening.

They stared at the clothes of the miller and his wife who were first out of the church. 'That's velvet,' said Gabriel, chafing his shoulder-blades against the porch bench because his own hessian jacket itched.

'You'd like a frock made out of that, would you?' the Mason hissed in his ear. 'A pretty blue frock to match your eyes?' Gabriel bit his lip and put his hands over his ears and did not speak again.

Directly in front of the church was an area of brick paving. In wet weather the merchants and their wives, arriving by wagon, did not need to muddy their Sunday shoes. The roots of the yew trees were lifting the bricks here and there, and all the cracks bulged with grass and weeds and little flowers.

As Gabriel sat in the church porch, a couple of young men came rushing round the church and began erecting a trellis at either side of the terrace, and draping the trellises in cloth. It was like putting blinkers on the church. A great commotion broke out as two huge carts arrived. A wagon larger than any Gabriel had seen before was struggling through the churchyard gate ahead of another, smaller cart, loaded with barrels, ladders, coils of rope and trestles. The large one had once been painted gold – patches of gilt still clung to it here and there like moulting velvet on a deer's antlers. It was open on one side, and along the edge sat four or five people, their legs dangling only about as far as the hubs of the huge wheels, so high were the axles. A weather-vane in the shape of an iron dog speckled with rust and gilt wagged at the top of a cane pole at one corner, with ribbon streamers blowing from its neck. A banner above the tail-gate had flapped itself to tatters and been mended many times, though its colours were faded by sun and rain and its pattern was indecipherable. But on the inside panels of the three cart-sides, brightly painted flowers and animals, stooks of corn and grape-vines as well as a rainbow looked freshly painted. Heaps of cloth and clothes stirred in the base of the cart as the wind made them billow.

The second, sideless, flat-backed cart sagged suddenly as one wheel dropped into a newly-filled grave, and several of the barrels spilt and rolled away with a hollow cacophony, banging against each other.

The Mass was over, but the townspeople did not disperse out of the churchyard. They stood about watching the carts roll into place on the brick terrace. Some burly women, who had carried stools to Mass, set them down again facing the church door and the carts, and settled themselves, hands folded in their laps, as if prepared for a long wait. They looked like broody chickens sitting on their eggs.

The empty barrels were used to support a huge

trestle-table alongside the two carts. The stage was ready.

'Did you never see a play?' said Squit, full of scorn.

'We live nine miles from a town,' said Gabriel, feeling his neck go red. 'I never went but twice.' He added defensively, 'I've seen a fair ... What is it, anyway?'

'Well, it's a play, isn't it,' said Squit, shrugging in the way that meant he was hoping not to be asked for more details.

'You mean it's a game?'

'No, a *play*, stupid. People pretending to be other people – Noah and Jesus and God and snakes and things.'

Gabriel looked sideways at Squit and wondered what nonsense he was talking now.

'Don't you worry your head about it, pretty boy,' said the Mason with a threatening, soft-spoken spite. '*You* won't be seeing it, will you?' And he picked up the boys by their hessian, and pushed them back into the church.

As Gabriel began work again, up in the roof, and his eyelids and nose and hair and ears got clogged with the dark-grey stone dust, he could hear the crowd settle facing the stage. He could hear the murmured excitement, the shrill bleat of women laughing. Then the church door banged open, and a voice shouted in: 'We can't have you banging on in here ... we can hear you the other side of town. Come and watch the Mystery, why don't you?'

The Mason seethed. He looked at one apprentice, then the other. Their eager, hopeful faces seemed to sting him like wasps. 'There's work needs doing,' he snarled at the figure in the doorway.

'Look at it my way,' said the man in the doorway patiently. 'You can come and watch, or you can carry on banging and I'll take your chisel and your lads' chisels and I'll push them down your uncivil throat. Today I'm God, and what God says is, and always will be – evermore – Amen. Got it?'

And that was how Gabriel came to see his first play.

A row of women who were sharing a bench waved to him and shuffled sideways, making room. He squeezed in between them, embarrassed at the touch of their plump, creamy arms. They smelt of fresh bread and lavender.

''Course, they're not *our* men,' one confided in his ear. 'They're not locals. Did you ever hear of such a thing? Worthless outsiders, I dare say. But just look at Heaven. Isn't that a thing?'

He followed the direction of her eyes and saw . . . *Heaven*. He had walked past it on the way out of the church without even seeing it. At the top of a flowery hill, on a cloud as large as a toboggan, sat a smiling, sunburnt figure in a glittering robe, and reclining at his feet along another ridge of cloud, lay a fat, sleepy angel, his skirts billowing in the wind.

But Gabriel could not keep his eyes on Heaven, much as he wanted to. He tried not to look to the left-hand side of the stage, where a hideous head gaped, its fanged jaws wide enough to swallow a grown man. Its tongue lolled on to the stage, and smoke trickled gently but continuously out of the back of its throat. As he stared in horrid fascination, and the hair stirred on the back of his neck, the creature's eye cracked open, blazing green, and looked directly at him.

The women along the bench squealed and accidentally squashed Gabriel between them as they breathed in. He did not notice: he thought it was fright that had stopped him breathing. He could not understand why, a moment later, there was cheery laughter and a round of applause.

'Bless you, child, it's only a play,' said a woman whose arm he had grabbed, pressing his dirty face into her dress. 'That's the Mouth of Hell that is, where all the damned souls go on the Day of Judgement for being wicked. Gobble, gobble! Ha-ha-ha!'

Out on to the slopes of Heaven stepped a tall dark-haired boy. He put a recorder to his lips and began to play. And from somewhere beneath his feet, an invisible fountain of music burst into the startled sky. So magical was the sound that a tree raised itself up off the wooden platform. A big red apple swung from it like a shop sign. Some of the audience began to sing, but their singing petered out as a gruesome man/lizard slithered out of the gaping, smoking Mouth of Hell. His horned, scaly, hooded face peered out into the audience and grinned. He was booed loudly, and the woman alongside Gabriel took an apple core out of her skirt pocket and threw it. It hit the church door.

> 'Out, out, unhappy me
> Who lately thought to be
> The proudest of them all
> – Thrown down from Heaven to Hell!
> Once was I angel-bright
> The fairest golden-winged sight
> That ever you did see,
> But now, unhappy me!'

Gabriel opened his eyes and ears as wide as windows, and in flew sights and sounds such as he had never known – a man and a woman in red and white cloaks, animals and angels singing, and God Himself perched cross-legged upon the slopes of Heaven. When it came to an end, he could not tell what he had seen and what he had imagined. When the Devil described the fiery regions of Hell, it was both wonderful and terrible. He wept for the poor bare lady and gentleman, Adam and Eve, thrown out of the lovely Garden of Eden because they ate the big red apple. He knew what they were feeling. He had felt just the same, as the Mason's cart pulled away from his own little cottage and he looked back and saw his mother waving and waving and waving . . .

The woman on the bench thrust her apron into Gabriel's face and wiped his nose. 'Don't take on so, child. It's only a play. I told you.'

The play was over. The Devil had crawled, on his belly, back into the Mouth of Hell, with a lump of charcoal in his mouth. And the fat, billowing angel had gone back up to Heaven to sit beside God. The clouds had hidden them both from sight. Gabriel knew the story: he could not remember why, but he had always known the story. How many times in this first year of his apprenticeship had he seen stained-glass windows showing the selfsame story? But to see it happen – then and there – in front of his eyes! That was different!

'It's the most wonderful thing I've ever seen,' he whispered in the woman's ear, and she wiped his nose again with her hand.

'Bless him, but he's a good-looking little lad, isn't he?' she said to her friends along the bench. 'All those lovely golden curls. I wish I had hair as pretty. Who's he you're with? Your father? Thought not. There's none of his ugly mug in you.'

'Is that a fact?' It was the Mason's voice. One hand took hold of Gabriel's long hair and pulled him up on tiptoe. The other, taking hold of his jerkin, lifted him backwards clear over the bench, so that his feet knocked against a fat woman's head and sent her head-clothes tumbling. 'Big bully,' said the women, but they did not come to Gabriel's help.

The Mason carried him, rigid with fright, off the brick terrace, round the side of the church, and behind the big old yew trees. Squit was nowhere to be seen.

'Hairy little monkey. A sheep's got less hair than

you. You're a flea-catcher, that's what you are. How many fleas have you got in that ticking you call hair?' The abuse poured down on Gabriel as though he had stood under an open window and a bucket of refuse had been tipped out on his head. 'Well, I've got a mattress needs stuffing. And that hair of yours will do instead of feathers.' The Mason threw Gabriel to the ground, without letting go of his hair, and drew a knife out of his belt.

'No! Not my hair! Not my hair!' Gabriel put his hands over his head and pulled away with all his might. 'My mother told me . . . I promised my mother!'

How could he explain? How could he tell, in the space of a single breath, the story his mother had spent so long in telling – about Samson the Strong Man whose strength was all in his hair. 'Samson!' he screamed. 'In the Bible!'

The Mason knocked him face-down to the ground and sat on his legs. 'Samson?' He roared a vicious, tormenting laugh. 'Did she tell you you were a second Samson? Well then, I'm Delilah!'

No, Gabriel was not a strong man, even with his hair. But what would he be without it? The knife dragged once through his curls with a rasping noise, and already he felt his legs powerless to move where the Mason sat on them. Would he be paralysed? Limp, like a dead chicken? Already he could not feel his feet. He opened his mouth to scream but all that came out was a reedy croak. Already his voice was weak. 'Not my hair! *Please not my hair!*'

Suddenly the yew trees gave a convulsive shiver and someone from the audience, strolling away from the play, poked his head through the low branches. He saw the Mason pulling back Gabriel's head and he saw the knife. 'Hey! Murder! There's a knave here cutting a lad's throat!'

'No!' said the Mason and sprang to his feet.

That was the last Gabriel heard. He dug his toes into the soft soil and sprinted away down the side of the church.

It was like his nightmares when demons were chasing him, and his feet were wading through tar. He blamed his cut hair for the slowness of his legs. At the corner of the church he took the skin off one palm, swinging round the end buttress.

All the way round the church he ran, and out on to the brick terrace again. Then, taking his eyes off the ground, he saw his way barred by crowds of people. The audience had hardly dispersed at all, though their backs were turned now. The words kept whispering in his ears (or was too much blood pounding in them?), 'Broken bond! Broken bond! Broken bond!'

Every moment he expected the Mason to grab him from behind, wielding his knife. He ran at the church wall, leapt up at it, failed to get a grip and fell back on to a grave. He turned back towards the church steps, thinking to take refuge in the dark building. Perhaps he could even plead sanctuary and live in the church for the rest of his life, safe from the punishment of the law, begging bread from the worshippers. He would starve! Who would help a boy who broke his apprentice's bond?

All these thoughts — so many unbearable thoughts — were swept through his head by the river of pounding blood. He found his route to the church door barred by the stage — the cart and the trestle platform and the Hill of Heaven and the monstrous, gaping Mouth of Hell!

Here was the space where he had seen such things as he had thought only the saints in Heaven witnessed. Such holy, biblical things! Part of him knew that they were only men dressed up and pretending. And yet while he had watched, he had been there — there, in the Garden of Eden. Surely it was a magic space, up above the cart wheels, out of time, out of place — a holy space that would swallow up a running boy and dissolve him from sight.

One foot on the spoke of the cart-wheel, over the rim of the stage, and Gabriel sprang on to the platform. It seemed a bare, splintery waste all of a sudden, not a garden at all. He looked up to the Hill of Heaven, but God was no longer perched there! And how could a boy who had broken his bond dare to set foot in Heaven anyway? Hell was the place for such a boy, such a girlish, loathsome, curly-haired, wicked, unforgivable boy.

The Mouth of Hell gaped at him; the mechanical eye stared at him; the throat gargled smoke. Beyond the gullet he could just see the Devil — what? — writhing in sulphurous torment?

On the far side of the church, the Mason strode into sight pulling along, like a great dray-horse, two unhappy-looking youths. 'I tell you, I was giving the runt a haircut, that's all! He's my apprentice! His parents pay me good money to look after him . . . All that hair . . . it's not healthy. It's spoiling his eyesight. Only today he fell out of the roof . . .' The youths let go, embarrassed, apologizing to the Mason.

Gabriel made the sign of the cross and jumped into the Mouth of Hell. The smell of burning pricked the back of his nose. He wriggled into the red gullet of Hell. Two hands from beyond reached into his armpits and pulled him through.

It was God.

'Get down in the barrel, son. Get right in and keep your head down.'

Gabriel had no breath to argue. One of the barrels supporting the trestle stage was pushed only half-way under. Gabriel was able to slide into it, head first, over the edge of the platform, and lay curled up in the bottom, as still as a hedgehog in hibernation.

After a year or a month or possibly half an hour, God's face looked in. 'What are you then? A cut-purse?'

'No!' Gabriel's voice came back at him off the sides of the barrel. 'He was going to cut my hair! I promised my mother! She said never to cut my hair!'

The face looked none the wiser, and shoulders

shrugged into view. 'Your mother's not stupid. It's fine hair. I could do something with that hair.'

'He said he'd stuff a mattress with it!' whispered Gabriel hoarsely. The fumes from the beer that had once been stored in the barrel were making him feel rather sick. When he climbed out, his legs were red behind the knees and as wobbly as two pieces of string.

'Who? That big oaf of a stonemason? The one who wanted to go on banging through my play? You're his apprentice?'

What was the point of lying? God probably knew everything. 'I ran away. I've broken my bond. Must I go back? Must I do penance?'

God did not seem to be listening. He was tugging at his lower lip and walking slowly round Gabriel. 'What do you think of this, Lucie?'

The Devil, wriggling out of the last of his knitted tail, wiped the shiny grease off his face and neck before strolling over. He said, 'Liked our play, didn't you, boy? I saw you over there, with the tears running down.'

Gabriel was galled with shame, though of course he could have expected the Devil to betray him. Guiltily he wiped away the girlish tear stains with the back of his hand.

'What's the matter? What's wrong with a few tears? The badge of a civilized man,' said the Devil, and wandered off in his short breeches, his ribs showing even through the dark curly hair on his back. He had thin ankles, too, and moved for all the world like a wolf.

'What's your name?' said God.

'Gabriel, sir.'

'Like the angel, eh? The Archangel Gabriel. Like name, like nature, so they say. Like face, like fortune . . . I could use you, son.' As he spoke, and then sneezed, his head was surrounded by a halo of white, just like a saint in a stained-glass window. Flour was emanating from his hair. It was an awesome sight. 'How would you like to join us for a while? Food and kinship. A job your dear mother would be proud to see you in. No more beatings than you deserve. And safe out of this town before your master takes it too hard.'

Gabriel's jaw dropped. 'But I'm no good! I only do corners and finishing!'

God seemed momentarily perplexed. 'You only do corners and finishing?'

'And cleaning up. And anyway, I don't have any tools!'

A fresh cloud of flour came sprinkling down as God burst out laughing. The more his hair lost its white, the younger God was growing. 'But I don't want you for a stonechipper! I want you for an angel! Keep your shirt clean. That's all you have to do. Keep your shirt clean and your mouth shut. I won't get you to speak yet awhile. Lucie's got a daughter. She can do something with you – clean you up. Whatever else you do, *don't thieve*.'

It was a strange commandment. Gabriel had never

in his life contemplated stealing so much as a flea from a dog. His mother and father had raised him to be a law-abiding Christian. But he did not mind God saying it, especially when he felt the kindly grip on his shoulder. It felt good.

The Devil had put on his clothes – dark, close-fitting clothes – and had come sloping back. Always placing one foot directly in front of the other gave him a slinking walk. He was told to put Gabriel in the charge of his daughter, and led the way. *He* did not put a hand on Gabriel's shoulder. 'I'm Lucie,' he said gruffly, 'because I always play Lucifer the Devil. He's Garvey, but you'd best call him Master. He'd prefer it. What he said about thieving – it's important. We need to be liked. We need to be respectable. One grain of trouble would gall the clergy and the councillors like a pin under a saddle. We're pioneers, boy, breaking new ground – planting new footprints on God's old Earth. There's none like us. Instead of plays being acted by the city craftsmen once a year, we've made a craft of play-acting. It's our profession. We don't do it once a year – we do it all year round – wherever the town councillors or the Abbot will pay us to put on a show.'

'I never saw a play before,' said Gabriel, to indicate in the politest possible way that he did not understand one word of what Lucie was telling him.

'Is that a fact? Is that a fact?' Lucie turned and looked at him with piercing black eyes. 'You liked it, though?'

'I think it's the most wonderful thing I ever saw.'

Lucie considered this and nodded his head. 'Shame to spoil it for you, then,' he said tartly, and walked off, leaving Gabriel face to face with the recorder player he had seen on stage. It wasn't a boy at all. It was Lucifer's daughter.

Izzie had the same pinched, dark features as her father and the same lank black hair but cut shorter. She walked round Gabriel with the same wolfish lope, then said, 'Hide in the wagon until we're out of town. You could get us all into trouble.'

Hell was a wooden arch with a cloth tunnel behind it and a simple catch holding shut the green eye. It smoked because there was a length of tarry rope nailed up behind the gullet which Lucie set alight before going on stage. God reached Heaven by climbing a ladder behind the wooden scenery. His world was peopled by half a dozen ragged individuals who had followed an assortment of callings, from seasonal shearing to thatching, cowherding to churchyard sexton. Mischief or discontent, a hard master or some family tragedy that made home hateful to them had shuffled together these jacks and knaves. All they had in common – Hob and Jack, Lucie and Garvey, John and Simon, Adam of Wendle, and the youth who played Eve – was a knowledge of the words of the Mysteries, some or all. Their affection for the plays varied. Some were there because, well, elsewhere they would starve. Some would have starved rather than give up the playing. The music was played by two musicians,

Rolande and Ydrys, sitting cross-legged under the cart with a hurdy-gurdy, a reed-pipe, a drum and a shawm, all hidden from sight by a straw bale. On a windy day, guy ropes were needed to hold the flat scenery upright.

Gabriel quickly discovered why a replacement was needed for the angel. They left behind the pot-bellied shearer who had played him previously. They left him slumped in a drunken stupor against the church wall. Lucie forced a penny into his soft, sleeping palm, dumped his shearing tools in his lap, and pulled his cap down over his face in the hope that nobody would recognize him for one of the players.

In the next town the Abbot politely told them they were not wanted. The craftsmen of the local Guilds had been performing a play on the Feast of Corpus Christi for eighty years. No outsiders could do it better, and the city's working men and women were too busy to waste another day in idleness.

'In the west, the Guildsmen threw stones,' said Izzie. 'When once we've been to a place, we're liked. You liked us.'

She had a bald, stark way of speaking, never looking Gabriel in the eye but staring over his shoulder with a slight frown creasing her curd-yellow forehead. Before Gabriel acted for the first time, she spent hours brushing his hair and fluffing it out with a hazel twig into a frizzy golden cloud, quite indifferent to his squeaks and ouches. It was as if she were arranging flowers or carding wool. It was just one of her many tasks.

She made his costume, cutting down a white linen

shirt and fitting it tight up round the neck. Nobody asked her to make it. She made all the costumes. It was one of her jobs. Her father left things with her for mending, like a sheep leaves its wool on a fence, in passing. She always had some piece of sewing stuck in her belt while she cooked. (Preparing meals for the players was another of her jobs.) She washed down the horses if they started to look or smell disreputable. So she washed down Gabriel on the day he first played an angel.

The ladder trembled as soon as he put one bare foot on it. He stood there, one foot up, one foot down, and watched the top of the ladder bounce against the rickety scenery. He was mesmerized.

'Is that ladder nervous again?' said a quiet voice behind him. 'You'd think it would have stopped shaking by now. But no. Every time a new player sets foot on it, it starts to shake. Pay it no heed.' And a green-gloved hand reached over his shoulder to hold the ladder firm. Gabriel turned and looked straight into Lucie's green-stained face glistening with grease; a leather forked tongue was clenched between his teeth, and his black hair was slicked down with water in front of the green knitted hood. Gabriel went up the ladder two rungs at a time, and stood sweating behind his cloud. All he could hear was his heart beating. Perhaps the audience had picked up their stools and gone home. He was not sorry.

After Izzie finished playing her recorder, it was her job to loosen off the ropes and allow the scenery clouds to flop forwards on their hinges, revealing God and all His angels . . . God and His angel. The cloud in front of Gabriel flopped down. He bent his knees, hoping to stay hidden.

'Aaaah!' A long, sentimental gust of female sighs burst from the audience. They were all faces – just a mass of white ovals, like a dish of eggs. Viewed from so high up, their bodies were foreshortened and hidden by the faces in front. They looked so eager, so willing to be pleased. Gabriel put his flat trumpet to his lips and pretended to blow – and, underneath the cart, a shawm blew a nasal fanfare: the timing was so good that it startled even Gabriel. Perhaps the small wooden area with its pulleys and flaps and tricks and traps and splinters and rags was magic, after all.

He saw the tree rise up off the stage and did not see the rope and pulleys that raised it. He began to know how God had felt, looking down on Creation on the seventh day, resting from making the World. It was all very good.

They were three towns away from the Mason. Gabriel had broken his apprentice's bond and no one had hanged him or flogged him or thrown him into prison. In fact the players did not seem to think it was important. They shared their food with him. They gave him a *linen* shirt to wear! And they never mentioned his girlish features or his bush of hair or the fact that he was so small and puny for his age. All they wanted was for him to sit still as a stone – to be a piece of scenery, a decoration like one of the stone angels he had watched the Mason carve, up in the roofs of churches. It was easy.

'Don't pick your nose.'

'Don't scratch.'

'Don't yawn.'

'Don't fidget.'

'Don't go to sleep.'

It was so simple, however hard Izzie tried to make it sound difficult with all her 'don'ts'. Perhaps she did not realize how easy it was to sit perfectly still while you studied the faces one by one of the people in the audience, imagining their names, learned the words of the speaking players, and then – best of all! – played the Wishing Game. He saved up the Wishing Game till last, and then he let his imagination loose.

One day the players would drive through country-side that looked dimly familiar. They would set up the stage among buildings he felt he somehow knew. The audience would gather, one particular yeoman turning aside, out of curiosity, to see these strange outsiders everyone was talking about. The yeoman's wife would tussle for a good place to set down her stool. The chatter would die away. The music would start. Then, seeing the hinged clouds fold down to reveal God and all His angels, the wife would look once and look again and stand up and point and clutch her apron to her mouth . . . And the people round about would tug at her and shout, 'Sit down, Missus!' But she would refuse and say, 'But it's *Gabriel*. It's my Gabriel! Father! Look up yonder. It's our Gabriel and he's an *angel*!'

He would not wave when his mother spotted him. He would just smile and dip his head a little, and she would have to wait until the very end to be reunited with him. They would see how still he could sit!

Why shouldn't it happen? More extraordinary things had happened! One month ago, each new day had lain in wait to ambush Gabriel: he had woken up cringing. Now he was fed and clothed just for sitting still, and crowds looked at him and sighed – 'Aaaah!' There was nothing to be afraid of, except perhaps Lucie. (No one who looked so evil could be quite safe.) But Garvey had a big, round, jolly face. Gabriel could shelter in God's good grace.

Such a weight of worry and terror and contempt had been lifted off his shoulders that he sometimes thought, when the end-music started up beneath the wagon and the audience began to toss like a field of corn, that he could spread his arms, if he wanted, and soar off his ledge, above their heads and round the church tower. As free as a bird. By the time he reached the bottom of the ladder, he was almost laughing out loud with happiness.

'What's so funny?' said Lucifer's daughter (whose job it was to foot the ladder).

'Do you never want to be one of the players, Izzie?' said Gabriel.

She shot him a glance which made him sorry for

asking. 'Me? Haven't I got enough to do without learning words?'

'But I don't say any words!' exclaimed Gabriel. 'And you're so clever. You do all kinds of things.'

For a moment, the scowl lifted entirely off Izzie's face, and she looked suddenly very pretty and much younger. She breathed in to say something, but her father came round the corner of the stage. 'She's a girl though, isn't she, Gabriel? You don't have girl players. I mean, I've made her look as much like a boy as I can so she can play her pipe, but there's a limit to how much you can cheat the public. People wouldn't stand for it. Come with me, boy.'

The scowl settled back on to Izzie's forehead. She bustled away again, harassed and busy. Lucie sloughed his snake's skin and padded into the church building alongside this particular stage, with Gabriel's wrist in one hand. Such a long, bony hand. Gabriel shivered in that grip and in the cold air inside the church. But when he looked back over his shoulder for help, Garvey too had descended his ladder and was following them into the nave. It would be all right if God was there.

'Can you sing, boy?' said Lucie.

'Sing, sir? In church?'

Was it a temptation? Was Lucie tempting him, to see if he would sin, like King David in the Bible who danced and sang in church? Gabriel looked at Garvey for advice. Garvey only nodded and said, 'Go on, son. Sing.'

'Sing, sir? Like the monks?'

'However you like. Just sing.'

So Gabriel sang the first thing that came into his head – loudly:

> *'Summer is a-coming in*
> *Loudly sing cuckoo!*
> *Groweth seed and bloweth mead*
> *And spring the woods anew*
> *Sing cuckoo! Sing cuckoo!'*

'Holy Jesus and Mary, he's terrible,' said Garvey.

Gabriel suddenly remembered the words of the second verse, and breathed in to begin it. But Garvey clapped a hand over his mouth. 'Never mind, boy. You do a grand job of sitting still.'

He looked disparagingly at Lucie who shrugged and said, 'It was just an idea.'

When they went back outside, Izzie had almost finished packing away the props. It was one of her jobs.

William Holds the Stage

RICHMAL CROMPTON

It was an old boy of William's school, called Mr Welbecker, who with well-intentioned but mistaken enthusiasm offered a prize to the form that should act a scene from Shakespeare most successfully. The old boy in question had written an article on Shakespeare which had appeared in the columns of the local press, and, being a man of more means than discernment, thought it well to commemorate his intellectual achievement and immortalize his name by instituting the Welbecker Shakespeare Acting Shield in his old school.

The headmaster and the staff received his offer with conventional gratitude but without enthusiasm. Several of the senior members of the staff were heard to express a wish that that fool Welbecker could have the trouble of organizing the thing himself, adding that he jolly well wouldn't do it more than once. The junior staff expressed all this more simply and forcibly by saying that the blighter ought to be hung. To make matters worse, the blighter arrived at the school one morning, unheralded and unexpected, armed with innumerable copies of his article on Shakespeare, privately printed and bound in white vellum with gold lettering, and, after distributing them broadcast, offered to give a lecture on Shakespeare to the school. The headmaster hastily said that it was impossible to arrange for him to give a lecture to the school. He said politely and unblushingly that he was sure that it would be a deep disappointment to the boys, but that the routine of the school would not allow of it on that particular day. The author offered to come another time when arrangements could be made beforehand. The headmaster replied evasively that he would see about it.

It was at this moment that the second master came in to ask what was to be done about IIIa, explaining that the master who should be teaching it had suddenly been taken ill. He implied in discreet, well-chosen words that IIIa was engaged in raising Cain in their form-room and that no one within a mile of them could hear himself speak. The headmaster raised a hand to his head wearily, then his eye fell upon the Shakespearian author, and he brightened.

'Perhaps you'd give your lecture on Shakespeare to IIIa,' he suggested suavely.

'It's young Brown and that set,' murmured the second master warningly. The headmaster's expression brightened still further. So might a man look who was sending his bitterest enemy unarmed and un-suspecting into a lions' den.

'Splendid!' he said heartily, 'splendid! I'm sure they'll find your lecture most interesting, Welbecker. *Good* morning. I hope to see you, of course, before you go.'

A sudden silence – a silence of interest and surprise – greeted the entry of Mr Welbecker into the class-room of IIIa.

'Now, boys,' he said breezily, 'I want to give you a little talk about Shakespeare, and I want you to ask me questions freely, because I'm – er – well, I'm what you might call an expert on the subject. I've written a little book, some copies of which I have with me now, and which I'm going to give to the boys who seem to me to show the most intelligence. I'm sure that they will always be among your greatest treasures, because – well, it isn't *everyone* who can write a book, you know, is it?'

'I've written a book,' put in William nonchalantly.

'Perhaps,' said Mr Welbecker, smiling tolerantly, 'but you've not had it published, have you?'

'No,' said William, 'I've not tried to have it pub-lished yet.'

'And it wasn't on Shakespeare, was it?' said Mr Welbecker, smiling still more tolerantly.

'No,' said William. 'It was about someone a jolly sight more int'restin' than Shakespeare. It was about a pirate called Dick of the Bloody Hand, an' he started off in search of adventure an' he came to –'

'Yes,' said Mr Welbecker hastily, 'but I just want to tell you a little about Shakespeare first. Now the theory I incline to is that Bacon wrote the plays of Shakespeare.'

'I wrote a play once,' said William, 'and people acted it, but they all forgot their parts, so it didn't come to much, but it was a jolly fine play all the same.'

'I wish you wouldn't keep interrupting,' said Mr Welbecker testily.

'I thought you said we could ask questions,' said William.

'Yes, I did, but you're not asking questions.'

'I know I'm not,' said William, 'but I don't see any difference in asking a question and telling you something int'restin'.'

Most of the class had by now settled down to their own devices – quiet or otherwise. William was the only one who seemed to be taking any interest in the lecture or the lecturer. William, on the strength of his play and story, considered himself a literary character, and was quite willing to give a hearing to a brother artist.

'Well,' said Mr Welbecker, assuming his lecturer's manner, gazing round at his audience, and returning at last reluctantly to William, 'I repeat that I incline to the theory that the plays of Shakespeare were written by Bacon.'

'How could they be?' said William.

'I've already said that I wished you wouldn't keep interrupting,' snapped the lecturer.

'That *was* a question,' said William triumphantly. 'You can't say that wasn't a question, and you said we could ask questions. How could that other man Ham –'

'I said Bacon.'

'Well, it's nearly the same,' said William. 'Well, how could this man Bacon write them if Shakespeare wrote them?'

'Ah, but you see I don't believe that Shakespeare did write them,' said Mr Welbecker mysteriously.

'Well, why's he got his name printed on all the books then?' said William. 'He must've told the printers he did, or they wouldn't put his name on, an' he ought to know. An' if this other man Eggs –'

'I said Bacon,' snapped Mr Welbecker again.

'Well, Bacon then,' said William, 'well, if this man Bacon wrote them, they wouldn't put this man Shakespeare's name on the books. They wouldn't be allowed to. They'd get put in prison for it. The only way he could have done it was by poisoning this man Shakespeare and then stealing his plays. That's what I'd have done, anyway, if I'd been him, and I'd wanted to say I'd written them.'

'That's all nonsense,' said Mr Welbecker sharply. 'Of course I'm willing to admit that it's an open question.' Then, returning to his breezy manner and making an unsuccessful attempt to enlarge his audience: 'Now, boys, I want you all please to listen to me –'

No one responded. Those who were playing

noughts and crosses continued to play noughts and crosses. Those who were engaged in mimic battles, the ammunition of which consisted in pellets of blotting-paper soaked in ink, continued to be so engaged. Those who were playing that game of cricket in which a rubber represents the ball and a ruler the bat remained engrossed in it. The boy who was drawing low-pitched but irritating sounds from a whistle continued to draw low-pitched but irritating sounds from a whistle. Dejectedly Mr Welbecker returned to his sole auditor.

'I want first to tell you the story of the play of which you are all going to act a scene for the shield that I am presenting,' he said. 'There was a man called Hamlet –'

'You just said he was called Bacon,' said William.

'I did *not* say he was called Bacon,' snapped Mr Welbecker.

'Yes, 'scuse me, you did,' said William politely. 'When I called him Ham you said it was Bacon, and now you're calling him Ham yourself.'

'This was a different man,' said Mr Welbecker. '*Listen!* This man was called Hamlet and his uncle had killed his father because he wanted to marry his mother.'

'What did he want to marry his mother for?' said William. 'I've never heard of anyone wanting to marry their mother.'

'It was *Hamlet's* mother he wanted to marry.'

'Oh, that man that you think wrote the plays.'

'No, that was Bacon.'

'You said it was Ham a minute ago. Whenever I say it's Bacon you say it's Ham, and whenever I say it's Ham you say it's Bacon. I don't think you know *which* his name was.'

'Will you *listen!*' said the distraught lecturer. 'This man Hamlet decided to kill his uncle.'

'Why?'

'I've told you. Because his uncle had killed his father.'

'Whose father?'

'*Hamlet's.* There's a beautiful girl in the play called Ophelia, and Hamlet had once wanted to marry her.'

'You just said he wanted to marry his mother.'

'I did *not.* I wish you'd listen. Then he went mad, and this girl fell into the river. It was supposed to be an accident, but probably –'

'He pushed her in,' supplied William.

'*Who* pushed her?' demanded Mr Welbecker irritably.

'I thought you were going to say that that man Bacon pushed her in.'

'*Hamlet,* you mean.'

'I tell you what,' said William confidingly, 'let's say Eggs for both of them. Then we shan't get so muddled. Eggs means whichever of them it was.'

'Rubbish!' exploded the lecturer. 'Listen – I'll begin all over again.' But just at that minute the bell rang, and the headmaster entered the room. Immediately whistle, rubbers, rulers, noughts and crosses and pellets vanished as if by magic, and twenty-five earnest, attentive faces were turned towards the lecturer. So intent were they on the lecture that apparently they were unaware that the headmaster had entered the room, for not one turned in his direction.

'This is the end of the period, Welbecker,' said the headmaster. 'A thousand thanks for your help and your most interesting lecture. I'm sure you've enjoyed it tremendously, haven't you, boys?'

A thunder of applause bore tribute to their enjoyment.

'Now,' continued the headmaster rather maliciously, 'I want one of you to give me a short account of Mr Welbecker's lecture. Let any one of you who thinks he can do so put up his hand.'

Only one hand went up, and it was William's.

'Well, Brown?' said the headmaster.

'Please, sir, he told us that he thinks that the plays of Shakespeare were really written by a man called Ham and that Shakespeare poisoned this man called Ham and stole the plays and then pretended he'd written them. And then a man called Bacon pushed a woman into a pond because he wanted to marry his mother. And there's a man called Eggs, but I've forgotten what he did except that –'

Mr Welbecker's complexion had assumed a greenish hue.

'That will do, Brown,' said the headmaster very quietly.

★

Despite this contretemps, the preparations for the Shakespeare acting competition continued apace. Mr Welbecker had chosen Act III, Scene I, to be acted for the Shield. The parts of the Queen and Ophelia were to be played by boys, 'as was the custom in Shakespeare's time,' said Mr Welbecker, who seemed to cherish a pathetic delusion that no one had ever known anything about Shakespeare before his article appeared in the local press.

'I'm not going to be the woman that gets pushed into a pond,' said William firmly. 'I don't mind being the one that pushes her, and I don't mind being the one called Ham that poisons Shakespeare. I don't much mind which of them I am so long as I'm not the one that gets pushed into a pond, and as long as I've got a lot to say. When I'm in a play I like to have a lot to say.'

His interest in the play was increased by the fact that Dorinda Lane was once more staying at her aunt's in the village. Dorinda was a little girl with dark hair and dimples, who was the temporary possessor of William's heart, a hard-boiled organ that generally scorned thraldom to any woman. Dorinda, however, appeared on his horizon so seldom, that for the short duration of her visits, he could stoop from his heroic pinnacle of manliness to admire her without losing prestige in his own eyes.

'I'm goin' to be in a play at school,' he informed her the morning after Mr Welbecker's lecture.

She gave a little cry of excitement. Her admiration of William was absolute and unmixed.

'Oh, William!' she said, 'how lovely! What are you going to be?'

'I'm not quite sure,' said William, 'but anyway I'm goin' to be the most important person in it.'

'Oh, *are* you, William?'

'Yes. I'm going to be the one that poisons Bacon or that pushes Ham into a pond or something like that. Anyway we had a lecture about it, and I was the only one that knew anything about it at the end, so they're going to give me the biggest part.'

'Oh, William, how lovely! Have they told you so?'

William hesitated.

'Well, they've as good as told me,' he said. 'I mean I was the only one that knew anything about it when they'd finished giving this lecture, so they're sure to give me the biggest part. In fact,' finally surrendering to his imagination, 'in fact, they *told* me they were. They said: "You seem to be the only one that knows anything about this man Eggs what wrote the play so you choose what you'd like to be in it".'

'Oh, William,' said Dorinda, 'I think you're wonderful.'

After this William, convinced by his own eloquence, firmly believed that he was to be offered the best part in the scene, because of his masterly recapitulation of its plot. In order to be sure of making a good choice, he borrowed a Shakespeare from his father, turned to the scene (with much difficulty), and began to read it through. He found it as incomprehensible as if it had been written in a foreign language, but he was greatly struck by the speech beginning 'To be or not to be —'. It was long, it was even more incomprehensible than the rest of the scene, it went with a weirdly impressive swing. William loved speeches that were long and incomprehensible and that went with a swing. He mouthed it with infinite gusto and many gesticulations, striding to and fro in his bedroom. He decided quite finally that he would be Hamlet.

His surprise and disgust, therefore, were unbounded when his form master told him that he was to be one of the attendants on the king, and that, as such, he would not be required to say anything at all.

'You just go in first of all and stand by the throne and then go out when the king goes out.'

'But I want to say something,' protested William.

'I've no doubt you do,' said his form master drily. 'I've never known you yet when you didn't. But as it happens, the attendant doesn't speak. By a strange oversight Shakespeare didn't write any lines for him.'

'Well, I don't mind writin' some myself. I'll write it and learn it.'

'If you learn it as well as you learnt your Latin verbs yesterday,' said the form master sarcastically, 'it'll be worth listening to.'

'Well, I don't *like* Latin verbs,' said William, 'and I *do* like acting.'

But it was in vain. His form master was adamant. He was to be one of the king's attendants and he was not to say anything. William's first plan was to feign illness on the day of the play and to tell Dorinda that a substitute had had to be hastily found for him but that he would have done the part much better. There were, however, obvious drawbacks to this course. For one thing he had never yet managed to feign illness with any success. His family doctor was a suspicious and, in William's eyes, inhuman being, who always drove William from his sick-bed to whatever he was trying to avoid by draughts of nauseous medicine. ('It's better than bein' poisoned anyway,' William would say bitterly, as he finally abandoned his symptoms.) Moreover, even if he succeeded in outwitting the doctor (a thing he had never done yet) the whole proceeding would be rather tame. If there was anything going on William liked to be in it.

It was a chance remark of his father's that sent a ray of light into the gloom of the situation.

It happened that this same play was being acted at a London theatre, and that the actor who should have played Hamlet had been taken ill and the part played by another member of the cast at the last minute.

'This other fellow knew the part,' said his father, 'so he stepped into the breach.'

'Why did he do that?' said William.

'Do what?' asked his father.

'Step into that thing you said.'

'What thing?'

'You just said he stepped into something.'

'I said he played the part.'

'Well, you said he stepped into somethin', an' I

thought perhaps he broke it like Robert did steppin' into one of the footlights when he was acting in that play the football club did.'

His father's only reply was a grunt that was obviously intended to close the conversation.

But William's way now lay clear before him. He would learn Hamlet's part, and on the night of the play, when Hamlet was taken ill, he would come forward to play the part for him. ('An' I won't go messin' about steppin' into things same as the one in London did,' he said sternly.)

In William's eyes the part of Hamlet consisted solely of the 'To be or not to be' speech. 'If I learn that I'll be all right,' he told himself. 'I can jus' make up for the rest. Jus' say what comes into my head when they say things to me.'

Every night he repeated the speech before his looking-glass with eloquent and windmill-like gestures that swept everything off his dressing-table on to the floor in all directions.

As his head was the only part of his person that was visible in the looking-glass, he did not trouble to dress up more than his head for his part. Sometimes he clothed it Arab fashion in his towel, sometimes in his Red Indian head-dress, sometimes in his father's top hat, 'borrowed' for the occasion. On the whole he thought that the top hat gave the best effect.

'Are you *really* going to be the hero, William?' said Dorinda when next she met him.

'Yes, I have a speech that takes hours and hours to

say. The longest there's ever been in a play. I stand in the middle of the stage and I go on talkin' an' talkin', sayin' the things in this speech with no one stoppin' me or interruptin' me. For *hours*. 'Cause I'm the person the whole play's written about.'

'Oh, William, how lovely! What's the speech about?'

As William, though now able to repeat the speech almost perfectly, had not the faintest idea what it was about, he merely smiled mysteriously and said: 'Oh, you'll have to wait and see.'

'Is it funny, William? Will it make me laugh? I *love* funny things.'

William considered. For all he knew the speech might be intended to be humorous. On the other hand, of course, it might not be. Having no key to its meaning, he could not tell.

'You'll have to wait and see,' he said with the air of one to whom weighty state secrets are entrusted, and who is bound on honour not to betray them.

He had now abandoned his looking-glass as an audience, and strode to and fro uttering his speech with its ample accompaniment of gestures to an audience of his wash-stand and a chair and a photograph of his mother's and father's wedding group that had slowly descended the ladder of importance, working its way in the course of the years from the drawing-room to the dining-room, from the dining-room to the morning-room, from the morning-room to the hall, from the hall to the staircase, and then through his mother's, Robert's, and Ethel's bedrooms to the bottom rung of the ladder in William's. William, of course, did not see the wash-stand and the chair and the wedding group; he saw ranks upon serried ranks of intent faces, Dorinda's standing out from among them with startling clearness.

'To be or not to be,' he would declaim, 'that is the question, whether 'tis nobler in the slings to suffer

The mind and arrows of opposing fortune

Or to die to sleep against a sea of troubles.

And by opposing end there.'

Even William did not pretend to get every word in its exact place. As he said to himself: 'It's as sens'ble as what's in the book, anyway, and it sounds all right.'

The subordinate part that he took in the rehearsals as the king's attendant did not trouble him in the least. He was not the king's attendant. He was Hamlet. He was the tall, dark boy called Dalrymple (he had adenoids and a slight lisp but an excellent memory) who played Hamlet. It was he, William, not Dalrymple, who repeated that long and thrilling speech to an enthralled audience. So entirely did William trust in his star that he had not the slightest doubt that Dalrymple would develop some illness on the day of the play. William's mother had an enormous book with the title 'Every-day Ailments.' William glanced through it idly and was much cheered by it. There were so many illnesses that it seemed impossible that Dalrymple – a mere mortal and susceptible to all the germs with which the air was apparently laden – should not be stricken down by one or another of them on the day of the play. Dorinda met him in the village the day before the performance.

'I'm *longing* for tomorrow, William,' she said.

And William, without the slightest qualm of doubt, replied:

'Oh yes, it'll be jolly fine. You look out for my long speech.'

The day of the performance dawned. No news of any sudden illness of Dalrymple's reached William, yet he still felt no doubts. His star had marked him out for Hamlet, and Hamlet he would be. His mother, who was anxious for him not to be late, saw him off for the performance at what William considered an unduly early hour with many admonitions not to loiter on the way. She herself was coming later as part of the audience. William had a strong dislike of arriving too early at any objective. He considered that his mother had made him set off quite a quarter of an hour too soon, and therefore that he had a quarter of an hour to spend on the way. He still felt no doubts that he would play the part of Hamlet, but he was not narrow in his interests, and he realized even at that moment that there were other things in the world than Hamlet. There was the stream in Crown Woods (he had decided to go the longer way through Crown Woods in order to make up the quarter of an hour), there was a hedge-sparrow's nest, there was a curious insect which William had never seen before and of which he thought that he must be the first discoverer, there was a path that William had not noticed on his previous visits to the wood and that had therefore to be explored, there was a tree whose challenge to climb it William could not possibly resist. Even William realized, on emerging from the wood, that he had spent in it more than the quarter of an hour that he considered his due.

He ran in the direction of the school. An excited group of people was standing at the gate, looking out for him. They received him with a stream of indignant reproaches, bundled him into his form-room and began to pull off his clothes and hustle him into his attendant's uniform ('It's time to *begin*. We've been waiting for you for *ages*. Why on *earth* couldn't you get here in time?') All the others had changed and were ready in their costumes. Hamlet looked picturesque in black velvet slashed with purple, wearing a silver chain. William tried to collect his forces, but his legs were being thrust into tights by one person, his hair was being mercilessly brushed by another, and his face was being made up by another. Whenever he opened his mouth to speak, it received a stick of make-up or an eye-brow pencil or a hare's-foot.

'Now don't forget,' said the form master, who was also the producer, 'you go on first of all and stand by the throne. Stand quite stiffly, as I showed you, and in a few moments the king and the others will come on.'

And William, his faculties still in a whirl, was thrust unceremoniously upon the empty stage.

He stood there facing a sea of upturned, intent

faces. Among them in the second row he discerned that of Dorinda, her eyes fixed expectantly upon him.

Instinctively and without a moment's hesitation, he stepped forward and with a sweeping gesture launched into his speech:

'To be or not to be that is the question

Whether 'tis nobler in the mind to suffer –

'Come off, you young fool,' hissed the form master wildly from behind the scenes.

But William had got well into his stride and was not coming off for anyone.

'The stings and arrows of outrageous fortune.' (For a wonder he was getting the words in their right places.)

'Or to take arms against a sea of troubles.'

The best thing, of course, would have been to lower the curtain, but there was no curtain to lower.

Screens had been set along the edge of the stage and had been folded up when the performance was to begin.

'Come *off*, I tell you,' repeated the form master frantically.

'And by opposing end there. To sleep to die.'

William had forgotten everything in the world but himself, his words, and Dorinda. He was unaware of the crowd of distraught players hissing and gesticulating off the stage; he was unaware of his form master's frenzied commands, of the frozen faces of the headmaster and Mr Welbecker, who sat holding his shield ready for presentation in the front row.

'No more and by a sleep to say an end.'

The form master decided to act. The boy had evidently gone mad. The only thing to do was to go boldly on to the stage and drag him off. This the form master attempted to do. He stalked on to the stage and put out his hand to seize William. William, vaguely aware that someone was trying to stop him saying his speech, reacted promptly, and dodged to the other side of the stage, still continuing his recital.

'The thousand natural shocks the flesh and hair is.'

The form master, whose blood was now up, plunged across the stage. Once more William dodged his outstretched hand, and, still breathlessly reciting, reached the other end of the stage again. Then followed the diverting spectacle of the form master chasing William round the stage – William dodging, doubling, and all the time continuing his speech. Someone had the timely idea of trying to set up the screens again, but it was a manoeuvre that defeated its own ends, for William (still reciting) merely dodged round and behind them and unfortunately one of them fell down on the top of the form master. A mighty roar ascended from the audience. Dorinda was rocking to and fro with mirth and clapping with all her might and main. The unseemly performance came to an end at last. The players joined the form master in the chase, and William, still reciting, was dragged ingloriously from the stage.

Mr Welbecker turned a purple face to the headmaster.

'This is an outrage,' he said; 'an insult. I should not dream of presenting my shield to a school in which I have seen this exhibition.'

'I agree that it's a most regrettable incident, Welbecker,' said the headmaster suavely, 'and I think that in the circumstances your decision is amply justified.'

Dorinda was wiping tears of laughter from her eyes.

'Wasn't William *wonderful*?' she said.

It was, of course, felt by the staff of William's school that someone ought to deal drastically with William, but it was so difficult not to regard him as a public benefactor (for the thought of the annual Welbecker Shield Shakespeare Competition had begun to assume the proportion of a nightmare in the minds of an already overworked staff) that no definite move had been taken in the matter beyond the rough and (very) ready primitive measures meted out on the spot by the form master.

School had broken up the next day, and, when it had quite safely broken up, the headmaster and form master informed each other just for the look of the thing that each thought the other was dealing officially with William.

'It was unpardonable,' said the headmaster, 'but it's too late to do anything now that the term's over. I'll send for him at the beginning of next term.'

'That will be best,' said the form master, who was quite sure that he would forget.

Mrs Brown had crept out of the hall at the beginning of the incident and was pretending to herself and everyone else that she had not gone to the performance at all, and so knew nothing about it.

A fortnight after the end of term William went to tea with Dorinda – a magnificent cross-country journey involving a train ride and two bus rides. Dorinda's mother supplied a sumptuous tea, and William, watched admiringly by Dorinda, did full justice to it.

'Dorinda so much enjoyed that play at your school, William,' said Dorinda's mother, watching the rapid disappearance of an iced cake with dispassionate wonder. 'She said when she came home that she never laughed so much in all her life. She couldn't remember much of the plot but she said it was awfully funny. It was a farce, wasn't it?'

'Yes,' said William, unwilling to admit that he did not know what the word farce meant.

'What was it called? We used to act a lot of farces when I was young.'

William gazed frowningly into the distance.

'I've forgotten,' he said, then his face cleared. 'Oh yes, I remember. It was called "Eggs and Bacon".'

The Man who
Understood Cats

ADRIAN ALINGTON

[*NB In a pantomine the Principal Boy is played by a woman and the Dame by a man.*]

No, sir, I would never speak disrespectfully about a cat. I've seen too much. 'Deep,' little Joey Duggan used to say. 'Cats are deep creatures. People who think of them just as pretty pets are making a big mistake.' And if anyone ever knew, little Joey Duggan did.

I don't suppose you ever heard of Joey. His name wasn't very well known outside the profession. But he was a great little artist for all that. Animal impersonator. Cats were his speciality and really he was marvellous. How many years running he played the cat in *Dick Whittington* I wouldn't know, but every

Christmas he was at it somewhere, and nearly always he stole the show. I know that because once I played Dame in the same pantomine with him. He certainly stole the show that year. I'd like to tell you, if you've got a moment . . .

The pantomime was in a big provincial town. Bessie Bates was Principal Boy and she didn't like Joey one little bit. Dick Whittington's cat acted his master off the stage. Not that Joey ever tried any funny stuff. He was much too good an artist for that. It was just that when he got into his skin, Joey to all intents and purposes became a cat. You never saw anything so life-like.

His secret was that he really knew and understood cats. He was crazy about them and they were crazy about him. He was the friend of all the cats in the world, that little man.

I was having a drink with him one day, and sure enough the pub cat came strolling along the bar to Joey. 'You see how he picks his way without touching anyone's drink,' said Joey. 'Dainty as a prima baller-ina.' The cat came up to Joey and began rubbing against him, and Joey tickled him and made his own private cat noises to him, and it was for all the world like two pals talking.

Then Joey began to talk about cats in general, about how in ancient Egypt they had been worshipped, and so on. And then he got on to the what's-his-name* of

---

* *transmigration*: passing into a different body.

souls – you know what I mean, the idea that we all live lots of times in different forms. As far as I could make out, his idea was that he'd been a cat at one time or another, and that's what made his act come natural to him.

Presently someone called the cat and he jumped down off the bar. Joey watched him.

'Ah,' he said, 'if I could learn to jump like that, then I should be really good.'

As a matter of fact, Joey was quite a bit of an acrobat. He used to do a stunt at the end of the show, just before the finale. All of us principals used to come down the staircase, one at a time, to get our applause. But Joey used to come from the back of the dress circle, run round the edge of the circle on all fours, and then jump down on to the stage from one of the boxes. That always went big. Bessie tried to get the management to cut it out. But of course they wouldn't. It was one of the hits of the show.

We come now to a night towards the end of the season. A night I shall never forget as long as I live. We had a big house and plenty of laughs. I had a little scene with Joey in the first half of the show. Comedy stuff. He used to sidle up to me and rub himself against me and then roll on the floor for me to stroke his stomach. Then when we'd got all the laughs we could, I used to pretend to see a mouse. I used to jump on to a chair, holding up my skirts, while Joey chased the mouse off the stage. It always went well, but on this particular night it was a riot. Joey was terrific. He seemed inspired. No clowning – he just was a cat. Once I whispered to him through a big laugh: 'Great work, Joey.' But he didn't answer. He never let up when he was on the stage.

I didn't meet him again till the finale. I made my entrance down the staircase. Then Bessie came on and called: 'Puss, puss!' There was the usual answering miaow and Joey appeared from the back of the dress circle. He jumped on to the rim of the circle as usual, but he didn't do his run round. Instead, he jumped clean out of the circle into the stalls below. Somebody screamed. For a split second I thought there was going to be a panic but – and this is as true as I'm standing here – Joey landed in the aisle on his four paws as lightly as you please, and began to walk up towards the stage with his tail in the air.

And that wasn't the end, either. When he came to the front row of the stalls, he hesitated for a moment, gathered himself for a spring, as you see cats do, and jumped right across the orchestra pit on to the stage. It was like a big black panther jumping. I saw the conductor duck his head, looking as though he couldn't believe it. Well, when that happened, the audience went mad. I never heard such cheering. It went on long after the curtain had come down on us for the last time.

Bessie looked as sour as anything. I turned round to congratulate Joey, but Joey wasn't there. Instead, I saw the manager coming on with a face the colour of green cheese.

'What in Heaven's name is going on?' he asked.

'Joey has been giving the performance of his life,' I told him.

'Joey was run over and killed on his way to the theatre,' he answered. 'They've just rung up from the hospital. Seems the dear little fool was trying to rescue a kitten that had run out into the traffic.'

No, sir, I shall never speak disrespectfully of cats. Not after knowing Joey Duggan.

Acknowledgements

The editor and publishers gratefully acknowledge the following for permission to reproduce copyright material in this anthology in the form of complete stories and extracts taken from the following books:

'The Man who Understood Cats' by Adrian Alington from *Good Stories* edited by W. M. Smith published by Edward Arnold, copyright © Adrian Alington 1964, reprinted by permission of the Peters Fraser & Dunlop Group Ltd; *She Shall Have Music* by Kitty Barne published by J. M. Dent & Sons, copyright © Kitty Barne 1938; *The Glory Girl* by Betsy Byars published by The Bodley Head, copyright © Betsy Byars 1983, reprinted by permission of Random Century Group and The Viking Press, USA; 'William Holds the Stage' from *William the Bold* by Richmal Crompton published by Pan Macmillan Children's Books, copyright © Richmal C. Ashbee 1950; 'The

Acknowledgements

Poppycrunch Kid' from *Letters of Fire* by Adèle Geras published by Fontana Lions, copyright © Adèle Geras 1986; 'Hear My Voice' from *The Shirt of a Hanged Man's Back* by Dennis Hamley published by André Deutsch Children's Books, copyright © Scholastic Publications Ltd 1983; *A Little Lower than the Angels* by Geraldine McCaughrean published by Oxford University Press, copyright © Geraldine McCaughrean 1987; *The Facts and Fictions of Minna Pratt* by Patricia MacLachlan published by Harper, copyright © Patricia MacLachlan 1988, reprinted by permission of HarperCollins Publishers; 'The Greatest' by Michelle Magorian from *You're Late Dad* edited by Tony Bradman published by Methuen Children's Books, copyright © Michelle Magorian 1989; *A Swarm in May* by William Mayne published by Jade Publishers, copyright © William Mayne 1955.